"Heidi Neumark's powerful book will retain its importance long after Donald Trump's presidency. Neumark has the unique ability to bring together people and events that are seldom in the same space—consider her chapter, 'Bedbugs, Condoms, Frankincense, and Myrrh.' Biblical texts and church seasons intersect with politics without apology: 'It's remarkable,' she writes, 'that people who gather to worship in spaces with a cross prominently displayed become upset about politics in the sanctuary.' You will never say 'sanctuary' again without hearing her passionate plea for the church to take sides—based on the Bible—with those whose lives are demeaned and dismissed. This is a book many have been waiting for; hopefully, it will also be read by those who didn't know they were waiting."

— *Barbara K. Lundblad*
Union Theological Seminary, New York City

"Pastor Heidi evocatively defines sanctuary as 'an embodied way for dreams to grow in a protected space so that a different future can be born.' This book is a sanctuary rich with the gilded stories of beautiful people for whom the church or society have rarely offered safety, finding their way to healing in a community finding its way to Jesus in our ever-changing and brutal city. A beautiful, compelling vision."

— *Winnie Varghese*
Trinity Church Wall Street

SANCTUARY

Being Christian in the Wake of Trump

Heidi B. Neumark

William B. Eerdmans Publishing Company
Grand Rapids, Michigan

Wm. B. Eerdmans Publishing Co.
4035 Park East Court SE, Grand Rapids, Michigan 49546
www.eerdmans.com

Published 2020
Printed in the United States of America

26 25 24 23 22 21 20   1 2 3 4 5 6 7

ISBN 978-0-8028-7839-7

Library of Congress Cataloging-in-Publication Data

Names: Neumark, Heidi, author.
Title: Sanctuary : being Christian in the wake of Trump / Heidi B. Neumark.
Description: Grand Rapids, Michigan : William B. Eerdmans Publishing Company, 2020. | Includes bibliographical references. | Summary: "Reflections on living in Christian community during our current times of political division, dehumanization, and cruelty"—Provided by publisher.
Identifiers: LCCN 2020017616 | ISBN 9780802878397 (hardcover)
Subjects: LCSH: Communities—Religious aspects—Christianity. | United States—Church history—21st century. | Church year meditations. | Christianity and culture—United States—History—21st century. | Trump, Donald, 1946– | Asylum, Right of—Religious aspects—Christianity. | Home—Religious aspects—Christianity.
Classification: LCC BR526 .N4235 2020 | DDC 277.308/3—dc23
LC record available at https://lccn.loc.gov/2020017616

I dedicate this book
with deepest love and gratitude
to the Trinity community.
You embody so much hope
for me and for our world.

Para la comunidad de la Iglesia de la Trinidad
con todo mi amor y agradecimiento—
ustedes infunden esperanza para mí y para el mundo.

CONTENTS

HOLY WEEK

EASTER

PENTECOST

TRINITY SUNDAY

ORDINARY TIME

CHRIST THE KING SUNDAY

ADVENT

FOREWORD

I don't know what the future holds for this country. I don't know whether the causes of liberation and freedom will continue to unfold in the mysterious ways that they have been. I don't know whether the hand of a providential God will once again break into human history. *Simply put, I don't know whether salvation is coming for America.* I often wonder, is the project of America even worth saving? Is the often-maligned, abused, denied, policed, hijacked, and deferred American dream even worth dreaming?

I also don't know whether this criminal administration in the White House at the time of my writing this foreword will win another election. But I have to ask, does it even matter? The rampant white supremacy, systemic and structural racism, weaponization of executive privilege and orders, and intentional legislative harm to communities of color have been here long before Trump. I'm not even sure whether the next election matters as much as the revelation that, in a lot of ways, this is who we are as a country. This is us at our core. This is what the republic is now, a bloated empire with no regard for its citizens, pitting those who don't know they are in a cage against those it wants in a cage. In the question of what came first to the White House, white supremacy or Donald Trump, the answer is obvious in his rise.

Herod didn't create the throne of Israel. He sat in it. In the same way, Donald J. Trump, the forty-fifth president of the United States of America, didn't create systemic racism and four hundred years of oppression. *He was baptized in it*. From gorging himself at the trough of end-stage capitalism at his birth to wielding the outsized influence that celebrity culture gave him most his life, he is truly American in his rise to the greatest office in the land. That rise was built on the backs of the very poor, empowered by the wealth of others, and filled with overt acts of hatred.

I don't know what the days ahead will hold or where we will be as the people of God by the time you read this. But I do know Heidi Neumark and the people of Trinity Lutheran Church in New York City. I do know that in the early days of this administration, they did public acts of church and liturgy that were resistance. I do know that as a leader in the church, Heidi spoke sharply and clearly. She didn't equivocate or negotiate with evil. She named a thing what it was when many others in the church were too busy worrying about congregational backlash and retirement-planning. Maybe that is a product of the incredible community she serves. Maybe it's because queer bodies are held sacred in Trinity's sanctuary walls and sheltered in its basement. Maybe it's because, like a sower, Heidi has been spreading the Kin-dom of God wherever she goes. Not worrying about what folks deem the best soil. The "proper" soil. Just throwing the seeds of new life everywhere she goes. That new life is a thing you can't bottle or recreate, but you know it when you come across it in the twenty-first century church, and you intuitively know it is precious, special, rare, and needs to be cared for and nurtured. That it has to be allowed to spread wild, new life and growth to everything it touches.

The author and pastor and the community you are going to meet in these pages are all those things. If you are looking for hope, respite, courage, and a draught of the water of life, then you have come to the right place. You see, there are people who have labored long and wearily in this cause. There is a ragtag army ready to wage peace on the world and turn back the tide of oppression sweeping this country and, by proxy, the American church. It is rising up. Thankfully, some of those joining its ranks are Heidi and the community she serves. May the author's words bless you. May the stories within speak to the tender places inside you. May you find sanctuary in the current raging storm. May you still find ways to look through your own brokenness and beyond your neighbor's brokenness to the *imago Dei* in us all.

In the Name of the Parent, the Rebel, and the Spirit +

Lenny Duncan

ACKNOWLEDGMENTS

I thank my God every time I remember you, constantly praying with joy in every one of my prayers for all of you. Philippians 1:3–4

So much joy and so much gratitude:

For the editors at the *Christian Century* who have been ever generous in allowing my words to see the light of day, especially former editors Debra Bendis and David Heim;

For Don Ottenhoff, Carla Durand, and everyone at the Collegeville Institute who create a magical space of hospitality for writers and creative nourishment beyond compare;

For Chris Coble at the Lilly Endowment who stewards the gifts of many to undergird this work;

For the Collegeville writing mentors—Sari Fordham, Michael McGregor, and Robert Benson;

For Lauren Winner, the true midwife behind this book, which would not have come to life without her—I could not be more grateful!

For the people of Trinity—for every baby, child, teen, and adult I have had the joy of knowing. I am so thankful I get to be your pastor and that you have given me such wonderful stories to share;

For my Trinity seminary interns: Jeremy, Chris, Elizabeth, Paul,

Cheryl, Sarah R., Nancy (RIP), Haley Vay, Gretchen, Barbara, Matt, Analyse, Sarah G., Abby, and Shruti. And all the part-time students—you quicken my soul with hope for the church;

For the courageous residents and devoted staff of Trinity Place Shelter;

For my supportive clergy colleagues;

For Helen, ever ready with wisdom and encouragement;

For my agent, John Thornton;

For the whole team at Eerdmans—especially Trevor, Laura, and Linda;

And for my family—Gregorio, Ana and Katie, Hans and Abigail;

And Mia Rose—my heart's delight;

Undying gratitude.

Christmas

1

Putting Herod Back in Christmas

I play to people's fantasies. People may not always think big themselves, but they can still get very excited by those who do. That's why a little hyperbole never hurts. People want to believe that something is the biggest and the greatest and the most spectacular. I call it truthful hyperbole. It's an innocent form of exaggeration — and a very effective form of promotion.

Untangled strings of stars shone on every inch of our Christmas tree, a pine worthy of the neo-Gothic heights in the Trinity Lutheran sanctuary. It had been cut down, delivered, and set up by our good-hearted, nicely muscled neighbors—the firemen who work across the street from the church. Our fully costumed King Herod strode down the aisle, past the tree, to take his stage position among the three kings. With all the bravado of twenty-first-century Washington, Herod declared, "The beauty of me is that I'm very rich. And smart. My IQ is one of the highest—and you all know it! Please don't feel so stupid or insecure; it's not your fault."

The real Herod, who rose to become King over Judea in the first century, proved to be a paranoid, narcissistic tyrant known for massive construction projects, building housing, palaces, and an enormous wall. His ego knew no boundaries or controls and he lashed out at those he determined were against him. During his reign, he had family members and three hundred palace officials killed—and that was before Herod's deadly campaign against babies and toddlers under two, an effort to eliminate the baby Jesus.

For those planning the Three Kings pageant that would be performed in January, a few months after the 2016 presidential election, the decision to cast the villain was a no-brainer. A congregant with acting chops offered to play Herod and a blond wig was purchased. Herod's Trumpesque lines were delivered to us via Twitter:

> The world was gloomy before I won—there was no hope. Now the market is up nearly 10% and Christmas spending is over a trillion dollars!
>
> *When King Herod heard about the child (Jesus), he was frightened.* (Matt.2:3)
>
> Liars, liars! Fake news! . . . A baby king? I'll take care of these babies. No more anchor babies. No more immigrant babies. These babies come from broken, crime-infested countries! They are criminals! They are drug addicts! They are ugly! . . . How does my hair look?
>
> *Calling together all the chief priests and scribes of the people, he inquired of them where the Messiah was to be born.* (Matt. 2:4)

> I know things that nobody else knows. I know bigly things because I have a very good brain . . . but . . . well, I need to know . . . where to find this baby.

The answer comes from a girl in Spanish: "En Belén." Herod looks puzzled: "She speaks Mexican." Another child translates, "Belén means Bethlehem."

> *Herod called the visitors from the East to a secret meeting.* (Matt.2:7 [GNT])

> Take their phones. Take their pencils. Look for bugs. Do not record anything.

> *Go and search diligently for the child; and when you have found him, bring me word so that I may also go and pay him homage.* (Matt. 2:8)

> My Twitter has become so powerful that I can actually make my enemies tell the truth. . . . How does my hair look?

In addition to taking some creative liberties, our actors dramatized the biblical account of Jesus's birth. Having been warned in a dream to defy Herod, the kings left their gifts at the Bethlehem manger and took a different route home, an act of civil disobedience (an integral part of the Christmas story) usually ignored amid holiday wreathes and candles. Near the end of the scene, the congregation stood to sing "We Three Kings," but Herod's supporters interrupted during the final verse.

Make America great again!
Anchor (babies) Away! Anchors Away!
Trump is King!
It's too cold! Global Warming now!
Build that wall!
Build that wall!

Herod joined them: "The people following me are very passionate. They love this country. They love me. They are very passionate. We're going to make America great again. Bigly great."

After the rant, Herod and the protesters marched back down the center aisle and an angel appeared, warning Joseph to flee to Egypt. Other angels handed Joseph and Mary a hastily packed suitcase, and the shepherds provided some of their own bread and water. The frightened holy family raced down a side aisle to cross the border as refugees from Herod's hate.

Many congregations never hear this part of the Christmas story because the visiting magi and Herod only show up in the Gospel of Matthew and most pageants focus on the angels, shepherds, and manger that appear in Luke's story. But our church holds its pageant near the end of the twelve days of Christmas, on the Sunday closest to Three Kings Day (January 6), following the Latin American tradition that commemorates the journey of the magi. Because this festival is beloved of children, our drama stops short of the point where Herod, infuriated after being tricked by the visiting kings, "killed all the children in and around Bethlehem who were two years old or under" (Matt. 2:16).

For my congregation, our pageant featuring Herod as Trump was much-needed pastoral care, offering an interlude of comic relief and truth-telling in a season of daily deception, delusion, anxiety, and fear. It enabled us to take a collective, holy exhale and keep going, like the kings, by a different road.

A year later, the humor in our pageant was quashed. In August, we heard Trump's opinion about "the very fine people on both sides" of a white supremacist rally in Charlottesville, Virginia, that left one counter-protester dead. In September, a group of California middle-schoolers instructed to invent a board game chose the theme "border crossing" and named their game "Deportation Time." Despite one student's objection, their teacher approved the project. In October, eleven Jews were slaughtered at the Tree of Life Synagogue in Pittsburg during a morning service.

Soon after this barrage of devastating news, I attended an inter-faith rally with church members in Manhattan. An imam spoke of walking down a street in Harlem to visit a sick friend and being told by a stranger that he deserved to be dead and if he opened his mouth to say anything he would be. While we sat and listened to speakers from a range of faith traditions, somebody drew a swastika on the doors of a nearby Methodist church that was sharing space with a synagogue whose own building was under renovation.

My daughter Ana, who lives with her wife and baby in upstate New York, was pumping gas when a man walked up to her and said that Trump was going to send her back to Mexico. My husband is a naturalized United States citizen from Argentina, and Ana has his dark hair, eyes, and a skin tone that is apparently not quite white enough to qualify her as a true American. All I thought was, *Thank God my sharp-witted, snarky daughter kept her mouth shut; thank God her wife and baby were not with her; thank God that's as far as it went.*

The Bible evinces profound psychological insight when it introduces Herod's furious reaction to the birth of Jesus with the observation, "He was frightened." Where did Herod's fear come from? We don't know. Martin Luther King Jr. wrote a marvelous essay "Antidotes for Fear," in which he distinguishes between fear that protects us and fear that diminishes us: "Normal fear motivates us to improve our individual and collective welfare. Abnormal fear constantly poisons and distorts." Wherever it came from, Herod's fear was clearly the latter, as is the poisonous fear being exploited by the president.

Only God knows the details and depths of Trump's spiritual life, but what Trump says and does publicly disavows every core teaching Jesus set forth in the Sermon on the Mount. Where Jesus says, "Blessed are the poor," Trump brags, "I like money. I'm very greedy. . . . I love money, right?" When Jesus preaches and embodies love for strangers and those on the margins, Trump speaks of "shit-hole" countries and compares desperate people to animals whose arrival is an "infestation." Jesus embodies forgiveness and Trump delights in revenge: "When people wrong you, go after those people, because it is a good feeling and because other people will see you doing it. I always get even. If you do not get even, you are just a schmuck." Jesus welcomes children and Trump locks them in cages.

The church must take sides. The time for being nice and passive, fretting about causing offense, and fiddling over mild and nonthreatening proclamations is long past. While we equivocate, lives hang in the balance. We know that fewer people attend church and offerings have declined with no sign of an upswing. Church leaders wring their hands and worry over what this means for the future of our religious institutions. In one way, I am grateful to Trump because he makes it so very clear where our future lies.

The future of the church is in cages with children. The future of the church is profiled and choked and left dead on the street. The future of the church is hiding under a school desk and in a nightclub bathroom as bullets fly. The future of the church is with a Black, transgender woman mocked and shot in the heart. The future of the church is in the belly of a whale stuffed with plastic garbage and lying lifeless like the body of a dead migrant child washed up on the shores of the Rio Grande. If the church is not in these places of crucifixion, the church is not with Jesus, and if the church is not with Jesus, we are lost and we have no future.

The author of the book of Hebrews writes to people surrounded by such life-threatening places.

> Do not neglect to show hospitality to strangers, for by doing that some have entertained angels without knowing it. Remember those who are in prison, as though you were in prison with them; those who are being tortured, as though you yourselves were being tortured. . . . Therefore Jesus also suffered outside the city gate in order to sanctify the people by his own blood. Let us then go to him outside the camp and bear the abuse he endured. (Heb. 13:2–3, 12–13)

By suffering "outside the city gate" with those whose humanity is mocked, crushed, and buried in prisons, press conferences, and hateful policies, Jesus brought their humanity to the center, raised up with him. We, too, can find our own true humanity and purpose by following Jesus's example. Herod lives on, but Herod's defeat is already in the books. Though the church I serve is comparatively small and poorly resourced, we have everything we need to live in these days as the body of Christ, to be Jesus in the kingdom of Herod.

After twenty years as a pastor in the South Bronx, I accepted a call to move across the Hudson River and serve as the pastor of Trinity Lutheran Church of Manhattan on the Upper West Side. The congregation embodies the kind of mix you find on the subway—a wide spectrum of skin-tones, ethnicities, and cultures; people with jobs, looking for jobs, or relying on disability; immigrants from Africa, Asia, Central and South America, and Europe (though not enough Norwegians for Trump's taste), with undocumented asylum-seekers and DACA Dreamers; students from nearby Columbia University and Union Seminary; residents of public housing, rent-stabilized apartments, condos, co-ops, group homes, SROs, and some who are homeless; a seminary intern from a small town in Tennessee whose parents voted for Trump, queer couples and singles, people with white hair and walkers, teenagers with eyes cast down on their phones who proudly rise to serve Communion, toddlers and babies, including a week-old infant sound asleep in his *Monsters, Inc.* outfit. For a worship gathering that averages around one hundred people, we have a dizzying variety of dancers in our pews, and sometimes in the aisles: a stilt dancer, street dancer, tap dancer, salsa dancer, along with those skilled in ballet, modern, ballroom, and Mexican folklore. Some people like to dress up for church, but most do not. A year after Della began attending church regularly, she told me that she'd walked by our building one Sunday morning and felt drawn to come in. Despite worrying over her attire, pajamas under her winter coat, and the possible reactions, she decided to risk it and enter. She now serves as a member of our church council.

Others brave more daunting hazards. For a transgender woman to cross the threshold of a church can feel almost as risky and unknown as entering the waters of the Rio Grande, even when the church waves a rainbow flag out front. For a grandmother from Eritrea, raised with a rigid anti-gay catechism, to sit down and share her homemade *injera* bread and spicy goat stew with a butch lesbian who brought Puerto Rican *pasteles* is much more than a delicious culinary interchange. They talk about how they arrived at that table, sharing their journeys across varied geographies of fear. Being part of this community has turned us all into border-crossers of a sort.

At Trinity, a porous boundary separates our life together in the sanctuary where we meet to worship and our efforts to be a sanctuary for those who are endangered. We work to build a safer, more loving neighborhood, city, and world that reflect the city we await. Our efforts include an after-school homework help program, a month-long summer day camp, a shelter for homeless LGBTQIA+ youth and young adults, huge Thanksgiving and Christmas community meals, a Latina support group, and participation in the New Sanctuary Movement and in labor organizing.

In the same week that Trump named his acting secretary for the Department of Labor, a man with a long history of hostility to workers' rights, unions, and minimum-wage laws, we made a different announcement in Trinity's basement. Children and parents had inflated lots of yellow, pink, and green balloons. A banner hung between two columns wrapped in red streamers like candy canes proclaimed: "Workers United to Stop Wage Theft!" and every wall bore neon-colored signs in English, Spanish, and Mandarin with a similar message. Excitement cut through the thick, humid air along with the mingled aromas of Chinese dumplings, duck, sweet and sour soup, handmade tortillas, sweet plantains, rice and beans, and chicken in *mole* sauce. The many Sterno burners lit to keep the tables of food warm had the unfortunate side effect of elevating the temperature in a room already hit by a heat wave. Those who moved quickly to open the windows discovered that a volunteer group had accidentally painted them shut. More fans were located. Ironically, the organizing effort we gathered to celebrate was called SWEAT (Secure Wages Earned Against Theft). Workers from our community had advocated for the SWEAT bill, which would strengthen the enforcement of labor laws, for years. This very room had served as a safe place for labor organizers to meet and plan, away from the owners who defrauded them. Now, the bill had passed our state senate and assembly, and it was time to celebrate that victory.

Of course, the sound system brought in for the occasion malfunctioned and tripped the circuit breakers, but eventually everything was ready. Children stopped running around and playing with balloons to watch proudly as their parents spoke at the microphone. Speeches were made in Spanish, Mandarin, and English. We ate and listened, cheered, and clapped. Looking at some of the church members present, I knew that they would not have come out on such a hot and humid night if they had not already shared the peace and after-church coffee with some whose ability to make a living was at stake. We were all enjoying a sweaty, church-basement revival that restored pinched souls, along with stolen wages. One community resident visiting for the first time asked me if the sanctuary, meaning our worship space, was upstairs. I told him that it was, but I wanted to say that we were already gathered in a sanctuary suffused with love.

Through the pages of this book, I invite you into various spaces of sanctuary—not as places of retreat, but for the deepened resistance, vision, and transformation that these days, and the gospel, require.

2

Jesus in a Cage on *Good Morning America*

> Now you don't get separated, and while that sounds nice and all, what happens is you have literally you have ten times as many families coming up because they're not going to be separated from their children. It's like Disneyland now.

Along with everyone else at the church, our pop-up planning team had seen photos of or heard about immigrant children wrested from their parents and held in *perreros*, or dog cages, at our southern border. Trinity has few ongoing committees. Most people prefer to focus on specific projects with bounded time lines rather than commit to an ongoing series of meetings with no end in sight. In the fall of 2018, a pop-up team met to plan for Christmas.

We usually decorate simply with a lighted tree, poinsettia plants up front, and wreathes hung between candle fixtures on the walls. A nativity scene is set on the floor before the altar with the holy family in the center flanked by a donkey and a cow. Shepherds guard their flocks on one side and kings approach with their camels from the other. This year our pop-up team decided to place the family figures in a dog cage among the candles and holiday poinsettias, with baby Jesus separated from his parents and covered in foil to resemble a tiny, Mylar blanket.

I wondered how the children at our early Christmas Eve service would react to the unfamiliar sight of Jesus and his parents behind bars when I invited them to come up and sit with me, close to the cage, as I intended to do. I debated removing the cage for that service and displaying the figures in the usual manner, but after some reflection, I came up with an alternative plan. I ordered a stack of real Mylar blankets, which came folded in tiny rectangles about the size of a packet of gum. When the children came forward at the service, I told the Christmas story and asked what they noticed in our own nativity scene. Did they think the baby should be with his parents? Of course they did, and so we removed the family from the divided cage and put them together. Then I passed out the Mylar blankets and explained how they were used to warm people in emergencies. We opened a few of the small packages and shook out the full-size gold and silver blankets. It was the first time I saw Gerard Manley Hopkins's words literally flash to life: "The world is charged with the grandeur of God. / It will flame out, like shining from shook foil." The toddlers and babies, including my eleven-month-old granddaughter, Mia, were thrilled with the gleaming sheets and sounds of crinkling Mylar. I gave each child a blanket packet and suggested they might give it to someone they saw sitting or sleeping on Broadway, just one block from the church.

The members of my multicultural congregation, including many recent immigrants, appreciated these connections between the Christmas story and current events, but others did not: "You are a fake, a fraud, a devil worshipper, an idiot, a religious mis-leader, a MORON! Why do you even exist?" This is a dose of the vitriol poured out after I appeared on *Good Morning America* as an improbable guest along with Roman Catholic Cardinal Timothy Dolan of New York and Bishop Michael Curry, head of the Episcopal Church. All of us had been invited to discuss the meaning of Christmas with George Stephanopoulos. The conversation lasted about ten minutes and was edited down by half before it aired. My ninety seconds unleashed a furious plague of letters, emails, and social media commentary, all because, as one outraged news outlet put it, "On Christmas Morning, Lutheran Pastor on ABC Compares Illegal Aliens to Jesus and His Family."

Before the on-air discussion, George Stephanopoulos had researched my background and learned I'd written a book about my discovery of a momentous family secret, the fact that my Lutheran father was born a Jew in Germany and arrived in the United States in 1938 as a refugee fleeing the fascist violence that murdered my grandfather in a concentration camp. Stephanopoulos alluded to my history while noting a present-day global crisis of refugees. I spoke briefly, mentioning that I would not be here today if our country had not welcomed my father as a refugee. I continued on to recite the part in the Christmas story where Jesus and his family fled for their lives to Egypt, adding that when I see refugees and asylum-seekers at our border today, I see Jesus and his family among them.

Most of the threats and hate mail that landed on my desk came from fellow Christians:

> The majority of the horde at our borders are drug cartels, MS13, Coyotes, sex/slave traffickers & a multitude of other felons, sent to disrupt our country & our way of life. AND a third are carrying diseases to us—TB,HIV, Chickenpox. We don't need either—disease OR criminals. PLUS, these people coming now are nothing like Mary & Joseph, nor like those who came during WW2. They would die rather

> than accept charity—they wanted jobs & worked hard& learned our language. These lovelies come across our border with their hands out. These people are NOT refugees—they come for a free ride! And your recent refugee comparison is ludicrous! It's not unchristian to want to keep our country & families safe from crime & disease & to keep our culture intact. So please Heidi- How you've EVER been hired as a pastor is beyond belief. Please, put a muzzle on the hogwash you're trying to get Americans to believe—we're smarter than that, & we know EXACTLY what's happening at our border—an attempt to bring this country to it's knees, & we're not having any of it—or your ignorant speeches! You're a laughingstock!

If only I had stuck to a veneer of harmless generalities, a glossy take on the story with no blood, dung, or mothers screaming in labor or loss. Christmas is about love, family, a sweet baby under the warm glow of starlight, not children slaughtered by Herod, gunned down in school, or dying in immigration custody. But those would be alternative facts.

Epiphany

3

Bedbugs, Condoms, Frankincense, and Myrrh

Sorry, there is no STAR on the stage tonight.

The "STAR" referred to Trump himself as he opined on the weakness of the Democratic lineup for a debate. Our star was definitely on Trinity's stage, but it took a while to find it in preparation for another Three Kings pageant. The stage was a catchall for children's games, books, and craft supplies for an after-school program, garbage bags filled with brightly wrapped gifts to be delivered on behalf of the three kings, and several large picnic coolers that fit nowhere else. We found the star hidden in plain sight among the mess and covered in glitter. A year had passed since the pageant featuring Trump as Herod, and this year, we decided to follow a more traditional script, although most traditions do not involve bedbug infestations.

While I moved piles of costumes off the stage, a trio of young people from Trinity's in-house shelter found me and handed me a plastic baggie. Inside, a dead bedbug rested on a paper towel. The bearers of this gift asked me if I wanted to have it for evidence. Not really. The young, homeless LGBTQIA+ youth wanted me to see the source of their distress with my own eyes. I saw and I was distressed. It reminded me of going to the hospital where people want to pull off sheets and lift bandages so I can see their incisions, staples, stitches, and wounds. Words are not enough. I am called to be a witness of these things.

I thought of the time that Annie, our after-school program director, asked if I wanted to see the "used and full condom" she found on the floor while setting up for the children who would soon be arriving with their homework. She, too, asked if I would like to have her bag it as "evidence." It appeared that I had become an ecclesiastical CSI. Fortunately, it is not entirely up to me to remedy these things, though I can sometimes light a fire under those who do have the power to take the necessary actions. I sent a quick email to our ever-thorough shelter director and immediately received the following:

> Obviously this is alarming, problematic, and must end. And yes, staff will indeed have to remain and serve as "daily condom patrol." Quick question, does "used" and "full" mean there was semen visible inside the condom? I assume so. Or does "used" simply mean opened and not in the package? While seemingly a nuance, we discussed this matter last night, and several residents use condoms as homemade, free, hair bands to tie their hair back. (This is a long-standing habit many street and otherwise homeless individuals utilize.) This information will help us further hone our interventions and approaches to remedy this problem.

Maybe I did need to bag the evidence.

I am happy to report that the condom trouble was easily resolved. Sometimes the threat of embarrassment can be a good thing. As I guessed from its location, the item was tossed there from a bed after solitary use. Once the light of day shone on the nighttime habit, the offender was not likely to repeat. Unfortunately, the bedbugs were better at evading the light and required a flurry of effort, expense, and changed plans. I juggled the bedbug in one hand and some pageant props in the other, thinking through preparations for the following day's Three Kings play.

- Need to get bobby pins for the haloes.
- Yes, that is a bedbug.
- The frankincense gift needs to be taped back together. So does the stable wall but that will require electric tape, preferably brown.
- Yes, I am calling the exterminator as we speak.
- Were there bedbugs in the stable's straw?

In the evenings, our church basement doubles as our shelter and refuge for homeless LGBTQIA+ youth. It is a humble space and it's seen a lot of wear and tear since 1908 when the church first opened, along with derision, as noted in the church archives:

> We still have a definite recollection of the censure, the ridicule and contempt poured out over the little congregation, because it had risked to undertake a task that seemed entirely beyond its ability. We were a laughing stock not only to the total unbelievers among the Germans, of whom there were quite a number in this district, but members of old and rich congregations down-town spoke quite indignantly about our foolhardiness.

The mean-spirited reaction to the first pastor's plan to build the church is somewhat understandable, given that the congregation consisted of only five adults and seven children at the time. Such "foolhardiness" has since become a hallmark of Trinity. The plans to build a grand sanctuary succeeded. Now century-old, chipped columns downstairs hold up a starless ceiling, and underneath it, homeless youth can snore the night away in safety. The daily scraping of beds and tables, set up and put away, worsens the already scuffed floor, a sign that many have found rest. We sometimes refer to our church basement as "the manger," because love is born there.

The children arrived to get into their costumes for the pageant. Johanna played the lead angel, tasked with guiding last-minute angelic arrivals in their routine. She was six, but I detected a future pageant director in the making.

Our pageant's little lamb, Hendrica, spent the first months of her life in the warm and prickly manger of a neonatal intensive care unit, after a turbulent birth. She was lifted from a crimson sea as her mother bled out. Through a miracle of medical perfection and divine mystery, the two passed together from death to life. Hendrica's mother now adjusted her lamb's wooly ears. I thought of Blake.

> Little lamb, Who made thee?
> Dost thou know who made thee,
> Gave thee life, and bid thee feed
> By the stream and o'er the mead;

Hendrica will know. I felt certain of it as she reveled in her mother's arms and our organist began to play the opening hymn. In contrast,

I ached for the lambs torn from their mothers' sides by Herod's minions: Trayvon, Tamir, Eric, Dontre, Michael, Tanesha, Sandra, Freddie, Sean, Aiyana. I ached for all the lambs who gasped for breath, who bled out in the street, the lambs deprived of stream and mead. Several of the children in our pageant had mothers on the other side of our border and wept some weeks in church with longing. I ached for the youth in our shelter whose families had shut them out and refused their calls, even on a holiday. I ached for my powerlessness to impart a convincing faith to my own youngest lamb, now an adult. Could I have done something differently?

Hendrica's father, Dan, assisted in worship. Dan is a stay-at-home dad and an artist who takes found objects with designs others overlook: pieces of cardboard and plastic, patterns on the inner flap of security envelopes usually ignored and discarded. From these abandoned shapes, Dan creates arrestingly beautiful and provocative paintings. He basically spins gold from straw, as befits our manger. Dan led the entrance procession as we sang:

> O Morning Star, how fair and bright!
> You shine with God's own truth and light,
> aglow with grace and mercy!
> In your one body let us be
> as living branches of a tree,
> your life our lives supplying.

Era played the star. She had been asking me about this role for months and arrived an hour early to get ready in her shiny yellow robe. At seventy-one, nearly seven decades older than the baby lamb, she had also come through a harrowing birth. Her sister once told me that the flow of oxygen to Era's brain was cut off at one point in the birth canal. This dimmed some areas of Era's functional capacity, but sharpened others. One Sunday, when Era came up for Communion, she pointed at the bread and asked, "Is there forgiveness in there?" Yes, there is. "That's good because I sure need some." At one evening Bible study, Era announced that although she believed in Jesus and in life after death, she was afraid to die. "Is anyone else here afraid to die?" Era searched the faces around the table. "Who else is afraid to die?" Those who presumably had their full share of oxygen at birth sat in uncomfortable silence trying to decide what to say. No one wanted to make Era feel stranded with her question, but no one felt quite ready to enter the sudden, rarified air of her honesty.

The moment Era had been waiting for arrived. She carefully carried the star to the front and took up her position at the altar, which now stood behind the manger wall. As the three kings followed the star, we sang,

> Star of wonder, star of light,
> Star with royal beauty bright
> Westward leading, still proceeding
> Guide us to your perfect light.

Era waved the glittery star back and forth on its pole. Later, I would find flecks of gold on the altar linens and one floating in the wine. After the last of the kings made his way forward, and we sang, "Glorious now behold him arise," Mary raised the baby Jesus doll high for all to see. Her little brother sulked in the back and refused to participate because he was angry at their father's drinking. This father, like the shepherds who apparently were not expected to join in the census, was undocumented, a person of no count. He worked hard, for too little money and no respect.

Our pageant actors and actresses hailed from around the globe. Joseph was from the African Garifuna community in Honduras. The three kings were from Mexico, Puerto Rico, and Portugal. Gabriel was born in Germany. The other angels came from the four cardinal points, shining in perfect light. One of our little lambs wailed. The other fell asleep. Mine was home watching football. I prayed and prayed that his own epiphany is on the horizon.

The pageant took the place of our usual sermon and was followed by prayers. The children finished their performance, went downstairs to change out of their costumes, and came back up in time for Holy Communion. After worship, we had a fiesta in the basement. The person who promised to bring a hundred tamales never showed, so we made do. At least the three kings came through with gifts and candy, and now Mary's brother happily handed out the baggies of sweets. After the party wound down, Dan, the three kings, and a few others folded up the tables and stacked the chairs to make room for the beds to come out that evening.

The kings left plenty of candy for the incoming shelter youth to enjoy, two of whom were celebrating a birthday. However, the time for candy and birthday cakes would be delayed by a laundry marathon in preparation for the exterminator on Monday. Unfortunately, we'd been through this before. Our protocol required bagging and sealing all bedding and clothing and going to Miss Bubbles, our laundromat, to wash and dry everything on high heat for at least forty minutes to bake the bedbugs. The social worker on duty was ready with a pep talk: "We'll be dining on two different birthday cakes tonight to celebrate Victoria and Che, and the exercise we'll get from the cleanup will be much needed!" This is the kind of radiant cheer you want when bedbugs are afoot.

While the shelter residents were at Miss Bubbles, our custodian arrived to take the upstairs and downstairs Christmas trees outside to the sidewalk, where the city would pick them up for chipping and recycling into compost for local parks. The angel wings and shepherd robes and the gold and frankincense and myrrh had all been packed away until next year. Era had relinquished the star and allowed our intern to place it back on the stage. The church was quiet and dark. We've prayed our prayers and shared the peace and received Communion. There is always forgiveness in there and we need it. I am called to be a witness of these things.

4

Poor Doors

First of all, I am a great Christian, and I am. I am. Remember that.

The sky-high cost of housing here in Manhattan has sunk to a new, moral low. Extell, one of the city's largest developers, applied for the Inclusionary Housing Program, which supplies large-scale construction projects with generous subsidies and tax breaks on the condition that the plans include a certain percentage of low-income apartments. Incentivizing these developers by appealing to their bottomless self-interest seems the only way to persuade them to do what they should naturally do. Just to make it clear that no goodwill is involved, Extell's application includes a provision that the people residing in the more affordable apartments would have their own separate entryway—at the side or in the back. People have begun calling them "poor doors."

According to one spokesman for the luxury developer, "No one ever said that the goal was full integration of these populations." Well, the one who stood on a hillside and said, "Blessed are you who are poor" might have meant that, but what did he know about twenty-first-century New York City real estate? "I think it's unfair to expect very high-income homeowners who paid a fortune to live in their building to have to be in the same boat as low-income renters, who are very fortunate to live in a new building in a great neighborhood." I wonder, though, how great can a neighborhood really be when the other residents want you to be invisible?

The first time I walked around the community in 2003, the diversity manifest on every side impressed me. Trinity Lutheran Church stands on West 100th Street in the heart of Manhattan Valley, a neighborhood on the Upper West Side, bounded by Central Park to the east and Broadway to the west going up to Harlem. The church and parsonage face Frederick Douglass Houses, a large public housing project of twenty-story buildings that surround basketball courts, a soccer field, and playgrounds rimmed with benches. Here parents and nannies chat as children play, and the elderly can rest aching joints, set up domino games, catch up on gossip, and keep an eye out. Young men and teens stand guard, keeping watch for other things. Only in bad weather do the basketball courts empty of pickup games, tournaments, or solo players practicing their shots. The swings rarely stand still; toddlers get strapped in for a ride and older children pump themselves up and down next to a handball wall. The third-floor bedroom window of the parsonage faces the street, and long after I go to bed, I can hear shouts from ball games mixed with the squeals of children and the thud of a handball. After the children go to bed, the swings continue to rise and fall with the laughter of flirting teens.

Among the primary colors of the playground equipment, lavender elephants spray water from their trunks and pinkish camels kneel down for climbing. Their paint flakes off to show layers of orange and yellow underneath, not unlike the tall sycamore trees that flank the park. Those, too, shed plates of bark, revealing patches of pale green and creamy yellow smooth, inner skin. These trees have been thriving here for centuries and are known for tolerating pollution and other tough conditions of urban life.

Our street is also home to police and fire stations facing the church, and a library and city health department next door. Further down the block, across from the projects, stand rent-stabilized apartments with garden areas. The stores I saw on that first walk in 2003 were mostly neighborhood-based: a block-long 99 Cent store, C-Town supermarket, a Dominican bakery, and Ajo's Hardware, in business beside the church for over fifty years.

You could eat at a handful of Mexican, Chinese, and Caribbean restaurants or slide into an Art Deco booth at the Metro Diner for good food and blah coffee. You could buy churros and tamales from carts set up every morning and after-school dollar Dixie cups of coco, cherry, mango, or rainbow ice. A church member who taught an English as a Second Language class had told me about the many undocumented immigrants in the area, but I didn't yet know where they lived. Most of the public housing required residents to move here legally, and the rent-stabilized apartments only benefited the current occupants. Other available housing, though not at the high-end level, would still likely cost too much for recent, poorer arrivals to afford.

At the time, I never imagined that Extell, Trump, and Chinese investors were positioning themselves to become even richer off properties around the church. Fewer than ten years from my first visit to the neighborhood, the developers crushed all local resistance and claimed every square foot of buyable land in the blocks near the church. They evaded requirements for shared community green space by replacing pocket parks and a public tennis court with rooftop plantings, accessible only to those who lived in the luxury buildings they garnished.

As property rates rose, local businesses lost leases that now belonged to large conglomerates that could afford the steep price, mostly banks and pharmacies, or remained empty. I wondered why anyone would leave a space vacant for years rather than to rent it at a lower rate. It turns out that an empty store is nothing more than a treasure chest for tax benefits. More and more of these ugly coffers are popping up.

The head of Extell beat out Trump on a deal for some of the prized local properties owned by distant Chinese enterprises and earned himself Trump's fury and bluster: "This whole thing should be investigated. I don't give a shit. This guy is a total gross incompetent, he's an arrogant fool." Extell specializes in ultra-luxury buildings that have been called "gated communities in the sky," now with occasional "poor doors" on the ground, off to the side, and out of sight.

Like many, I am disgusted by apartment buildings with segregated entrances for lower-income residents. Yet, in many churches, the members enter through the main door on Sunday and the food-pantry patrons enter through a side door during the week. In the luxury apartments the wealthy have beautiful views and perks, such as a roof garden, gym, spa, screening room, playroom, pet salon, and lap pool, all ready to use without requiring a step outside their building. Lower-income residents who live in the same buildings, thanks to the Inclusionary Housing Program, are denied entrance into any of these facilities. We as churchgoers value our sacraments as much more than perks to hoard. Still, though we may not wish it, a class-based separation often exists between those who enjoy Communion in our sanctuaries and those who enter the church for other reasons.

On a Wednesday, Susan, a church member who made her home in supportive housing for low-income people living with mental illness, came by for a scheduled prayer session. Susan comes regularly for this midweek prayer session because the list of people she prays for is so impossibly long. Two years ago, she and I agreed that she would pick three individuals for prayer each Sunday and our weekly prayer group would take on the rest. Due to vacations, illness, and work schedules, that week's prayer group was just Susan and me. She once lived on the street, and her prayers always include many homeless friends. I often get impatient with the length and minutiae of her prayers, as if I had something more important to do than join her in attending to the souls she honors, and lifts from invisibility, with her petitions. Finally, after what seemed like one endless, meticulously detailed prayer for her long list of people, she looked up and said, "The homeless are seen as part of the landscape and scenery of New York like pigeons. They are thought of as 'its.'" Susan will never be guilty of that. She knows what the developers do not: that we belong in the same boat. In fact, the old word for the space in which we worship is "nave," from the Latin "boat." We are all richer because Susan brings her prayers and her wisdom with her each Sunday—through the front doors.

My husband, Gregorio, grew up knowing poverty deep in his bones—and in his teeth, having no access to a dentist (for which we now pay dearly). In his twenties, he moved with his family from the rural north of Argentina to Buenos Aires like many others looking for jobs that did not depend on faltering seasonal crops like cotton and sugarcane. They were part of a large migration priced out of housing in the capital city and forced to move into squatters areas often called *villas miserias*, meaning "towns of misery."

Before the 1978 World Cup, these *villas* were just outside of central Buenos Aires, close to the menial jobs the city offered, until the military dictatorship saw an opportunity to impress the sport's wealthy, international fans. The generals hired a public-relations firm based in Manhattan that recommended using bulldozers, which easily crushed the makeshift homes of thousands. This forced the inhabitants to move away, out of sight and far from jobs that now required a two-hour commute each way.

Obscuring poverty constituted only a small part of the New York firm's conquests. Not unlike the 1936 Olympic games in Berlin, hosting the World Cup provided an opportunity for Argentina to disprove the growing rumors of human rights abuses at the hands of the dictatorship. Argentinean leaders wanted to use the World Cup to repackage their country with a new image of "stability," and ignore that the games took place in a stadium less than a mile away from the infamous Navy Superior Mechanics School, where the junta tortured and killed thousands of people. The rational for those heinous crimes was that those who critiqued the government were undoubtedly all terrorists, a reasoning on the rise in our own nation.

Argentina was still under a dictatorship during the year I spent at an ecumenical seminary in Buenos Aires. In addition to studying, I volunteered with a human rights organization, Servicio Paz y Justicia. Some young women I met through this group invited me to move in with them in the squatters' area where they lived and worked with lay-led Christian base communities, requiring my own two-hour bus ride to and from classes in the city. This was also where my husband lived and where we met and fell in love. We go back to visit as often as we can afford to make the trip. Since I'm an only child and Gregorio is one of twelve, our two children have no cousins in New York, but in Argentina, they have dozens.

We last visited as a group of five adults: me and Gregorio, our daughter Ana and her wife Katie, and our son Hans. None of our relatives had enough room to accommodate all five of us, even on the floor, so we slept in the apartment of a pastor-friend in Buenos Aires. Every day, we left the grand avenues, gorgeous nineteenth-century architecture, and chic stores of the city and drove until we hit the rutted, dirt roads where our family members lived. We knew we were close when our eyes started watering and our lungs sucked in smoke from piles of burning trash. The government did not feel compelled to collect garbage in these outlying areas where many who kept the city polished and shiny lived.

The aromas of grilling beef, chicken, and chorizo sausages quickly overcame the stench of polluted air as various family members hosted us at one celebratory meal after another. At each home it was the same: hugs and kisses, happy tears, and *yerba mate*, the ubiquitous Argentinean tea you drink from a gourd through a silver (or silverish) straw. We caught up, shared stories and pictures, and took selfies. I was relieved that everyone embraced Ana's wife, Katie, as one of the family.

We set up enough makeshift, outdoor tables to seat a crowd of forty to fifty people. Hopeful dogs and children hung around the fire, waiting for the first tastes of the meal. At last, platters of green salad, potato salad, and bread were brought out, heralding the main attraction, hot from the grill. After eating, it was time for soccer. Every group we visited could field several teams and a large cheering section, just one of the advantages to such a big family. The games would take place right where we were, in a dusty yard or a short walk away.

This became the daily pattern, until the day something different happened. Our nephew Hugo had informed us that we would find a surprise when we arrived at his home. On the ride out to Hugo's, we wondered what to expect. The surprise turned out to be Hugo's brother, our nephew, Claudio.

Until then, we were the main attraction at these feasts. Gregorio was the son who made good, the golden boy living in New York, the city of dreams. Most of the family didn't understand how we who lived on an island of wealth couldn't afford to all fly to Argentina every year. But when we did visit, the joyous reunions outweighed all else. Now, however, we were going to be upstaged. The spotlight would shine on someone else. In the gathering at Hugo's, the starring role belonged to Claudio. I watched people hugging him repeatedly, patting him with love, stroking his face, kissing him, loading his plate with food, and filling his glass. Why this special attention for Claudio?

Claudio was not a son who made good. He was home on a visit from prison, where he was serving a sentence for murder. He may or may not have killed in self-defense. He may or may not have taken the full burden of guilt to spare his younger brother who was with him that night, but the details of that event were not particularly relevant. Claudio was twenty when he was arrested. His seven-year sentence would end in a few months. In Argentina, when inmates reach their final year of prison, they go home on monthly visits. The first visit lasts twelve hours, then thirty-six hours, and finally forty-eight hours. Claudio was home on a two-day visit that he'd chosen to coincide with ours.

It's such a sensible policy. The visits help people reconnect with family on the outside and adjust to life after incarceration. Hans was incredulous that these visits were unaccompanied and that Claudio was expected to get back to prison on time, on his own. But inmates know that if they return late, they extend their sentence. That deterrent makes the policy a successful one.

I remembered living in Argentina under the dictatorship, when a sentence to prison had meant that a person disappeared at the bottom of the ocean. I was deeply impressed by Argentina's new commitment to prison reform (although many of those who were imprisoned should never have been incarcerated in the first place, as is true for so many in our nation where poverty often segues into a prison sentence).

What I saw in the community gathered around my nephew impressed me even more. This group seemed to have emerged straight from the mount of the Beatitudes, where Jesus pronounced blessings on the poor and the outcasts, the president's cast of losers. Several of the gathered were missing eyes, one due to a fight and another due to untreated diabetes. One needed a cane to walk, one sat in a rickety, homemade wheelchair, and Claudio received the place of honor.

During my seminary year in Argentina, I spent one summer in Peru, where I had the opportunity to study with Gustavo Gutiérrez, whom many consider the father of liberation theology. At the time, he was lecturing from his soon-to-be-published book *We Drink from Our Own Wells: The Spiritual Journey of a People*. I felt honored to sit at his feet and drink in wisdom that would suffuse my own spirituality. Like his theology of solidarity, Gutiérrez was short and squat, close to the ground. He understood conversion as a call to follow Jesus to the side of the suffering, to love and accompany others in their struggle to undo all that systemically spawns suffering and poverty in his Latin American context. Many criticized liberation theology for replacing faith with ethical action, but listening to Gutiérrez made it clear to me that his life and stubborn hope sprang from the living waters of God's grace. He decried any theology or praxis that poisoned the water: "The denunciation of injustice implies the rejection of the use of Christianity to legitimize the established order."

Reading those words today, I cannot help but think of those Christians who support, by action or passive silence, an established order in the United States where white nationalism reigns and profits from keeping children in cages and Black men in prison, depriving millions of health care, and removing the poor from the visible landscape of the rich. In my notes from the summer lectures, I transcribed Gutiérrez's words: "The powerful spread death to protect the privileged." As I write this almost four decades later, a white nationalist has killed twenty-two people in an El Paso Walmart and injured many more. A few months earlier at a Florida rally, the president asked the crowd for ideas to block migrants from crossing the border. "How do you stop these people?" he asked. "Shoot them!" one man shouted. Trump smiled: "That's only in the Panhandle you can get away with that stuff." The El Paso shooter wrote that he wanted to stop a "Hispanic invasion of Texas." He spread death to protect the privileged.

Sitting with my family in Argentina, I saw a different order in the gathered bodies, at a table far from any conventional privilege. Prison had changed Claudio. He was no longer the cheerful, outgoing, funny boy I remembered from a visit years before. Then we had kicked a soccer ball around the dusty yard behind his home and he proudly showed me the trick of sticking his stomach in and out. Now, he was withdrawn and traumatized—so our family told me as they lavished him with love. As Claudio sat enjoying an after-dinner coffee and flan, served on cheap plastic but as delicious as any offered at a Buenos Aires *Confiteria*, I asked him about his experience inside prison. He didn't want to discuss it. "I'm surviving," was all that he said. And then he added, lifting up his downcast eyes at the people around him, "This is what matters."

5

That None May Be Lost

What you're seeing and what you're reading is not what's happening.

The daughter of a seminary classmate called me up and asked if we could go out for coffee. I hadn't known her parents well but was happy to meet their daughter, who lived in Brooklyn. I waited for her near Trinity at a small Mexican restaurant with great coffee. At night, the loud Mexican pop music favored by the staff alternates with *rancheros* for the gringos, along with margarita-laced laughter that makes serious conversation impossible, but during the day, it's quiet and rather empty, perfect for leisurely talks.

I was halfway through a strong *café con leche* when Suzanne walked in. She had long, dark hair, wire glasses, and a wide smile. She was an accomplished cellist and, to my surprise, a high-end call girl. I also learned that she was furious at her pastor-father for many good reasons. We talked about her family, her complicated mix of anger toward and longing for the church, her financial struggles, and her fears after a friend was almost murdered by her john. We drank several coffees and she asked me to include her on the church email list, even though work and travel for musical gigs took her away most weekends. I later learned that she left her riskier, more lucrative job and achieved international success with her cello.

Suzanne remained part of a group called The Red Umbrella Project, which describes itself as "conducting research about sex workers and the sex industry in order to better understand it, develop public education initiatives, and advocate for the rights of sex workers." Months after our coffee date, Red Umbrella was having trouble finding a site to host a service of remembrance on the International Day to End Violence Against Sex Workers, and Suzanne gave them my contact information. When I told the church council that I had received a call asking if we would open our doors for the event, they unanimously agreed.

Red Umbrella volunteers wrote the names of the dead on ribbons floating on strings hung between the tall columns in our neo-Gothic sanctuary. The event began with some of the gathered coming forward to speak of their experiences. A young college student told of being kicked out of his home when he came out to his parents and how he had sold sex to survive. A transgender woman spoke of the lewd remarks and snickers that assaulted her when she reported her rape at the local precinct. Another transgender woman spoke of her friend found strangled and hanged in her closet, among her sparkly gowns.

Two women I'd never seen before stood behind the altar, one leaning her head on the shoulder of the other. Together they lit the nearly three hundred votive candles that covered the surface of our holy table and wiped away each other's tears. During the candle lighting, those seated throughout the room read from slips of paper that had been distributed to each person upon arrival. Some passed their paper to a neighbor, unable to get the words out. The sanctuary filled with the names of the murdered, their places of death, dates of death, ages at death, all to an undercurrent of sobs. The naming went on and on, as we gathered fragments of lost lives from the shadows and lifted them into the light. Most of those named had died young. All had been sex workers. In fact, most of those gathered in the sanctuary for the memorial service had been, or still were, sex workers.

I have not walked in their shoes, and I cannot claim to fully understand their lives. I do understand that every human needs to know oneself as a beloved child of God no matter what. I understand that no child of God should ever be used, abused, violated, slain, or dumped as garbage on the margins of our communities.

Early in the planning of the event, one of the organizers asked me if we could place a table at the front of the church for the votive candles. I made a mental note to have our custodian fulfill the request. On the night before the service, the organizer checked in to confirm that all was ready, and I realized I'd forgotten about the table. It struck me, then, that we already had a table in front of the church. We gather around this table every week, the table where we remember the betrayed, broken, and bloodied body of Jesus given for us, the table where the fragments of that body make us whole. "You can place the candles on the altar," I said. "Are you sure?" she asked, sounding shocked. I was sure. I was sure that the lives lost were beloved by God. I was sure that the light that shines in the shadows shines for them, perhaps especially for them.

The sight of the two sex workers standing behind our altar, in a position usually reserved for ordained ministers and trained lay Communion assistants, made me reflect. In that moment, those two women became ministers of grace. Their faces shone with reflected candlelight as they leaned against each other for support. The women were signs of God's mercy for every person in that sanctuary. Everything flipped upside down at the altar, but isn't that what we proclaim every week? At our altars, betrayal gives way to forgiveness and life is offered to all in the face of death. To behold these two women at our altar was to witness a holy reversal where those labeled as dishonorable find honor, where those usually condemned to the margins preside with power. What did it signify if not a moment of Holy Communion? Of epiphany?

Many churches have lost the biblical pattern of outsiders becoming the bearers of revelation. After Jesus miraculously fed a multitude of people from two fish and five loaves of bread, he ordered his disciples to "gather up the fragments left over, so that nothing may be lost" (John 6:12). Jesus's words remind me of how fragmented we have become as a church. "We" are part of the chosen witnesses, bearing the gospel to "them," that none may be lost. Yet this very notion belies our own lostness.

How many middle-class church members can name five sex workers? Or even one? Any gang members? People living in crushing poverty? Undocumented mothers? Incarcerated youth? Most of us in the mainline church cannot, because we reside in a fragmented nation. Sadly, even our churches often mirror the increasingly divided culture around us rather than the gospel where every broken-off piece of the whole is gathered in.

Growing up in suburban New Jersey, I could not have come up with the names either. The only severe poverty I saw was on a mission filmstrip at church. No gang members hung on the corners of my street. If sex workers attended my church, I was none the wiser for it. I lived removed from major differences in class and race, but, thankfully, not from books that carried the voices and perspectives of others into my heart and mind. I remember the chill in my own thirteen-year-old soul upon reading *Soul on Ice,* written by Eldridge Cleaver when he was in Folsom State Prison, and *The Autobiography of Malcolm X.* Why would a white, suburban child gravitate to such books?

I've come to believe that my impulse toward listening to marginalized voices stems from inherited trauma. For as long as I can remember, I've been drawn to voices that many others ignore, deny, or stifle. When, in my fifties, I discovered that I descended from German Jews on my father's side, from ancestors who were hounded in pogroms and murdered in camps, I feverishly researched to learn their names and their stories. In uncovering my hidden history, I came to realize that the silenced cries of my murdered grandfather and many other lost Jewish ancestors have been calling out to me all along through the voices I do hear. My family was targeted for deadly racial profiling, and I was born into a heritage of white privilege. Both strands of identity wind through my DNA.

I've learned over the years that proximity and listening help us begin to bridge our divides. I know the names of undocumented mothers and people living in poverty because I live and work and worship where our paths meet every day. I know the names of sex workers because homeless people, queer youth, and young adults live in the church I serve, and many of them engage in sex work in order to survive. I knew sex workers in my previous congregation in the Bronx because some of our neighbors, and members, sold their bodies to get high or to pay for college. It was typical for people to say, "I'll come to church when I get my life together," and just as common for church leaders with similar histories to respond, "Church is for those who don't have their life together." Stories came out in prayer groups and Bible studies. Those who had attended longest opened up and shared their journeys first, encouraging others to do the same, because listening precluded judgment.

In *Life Together*, Dietrich Bonhoeffer wrote words that long ago convicted me: "So often Christians, especially preachers, think that their only service is always to have to 'offer' something when they are together with other people. They forget that listening can be a greater service . . . Christians who can no longer listen to one another will soon no longer be listening to God either." His words helped shape my own path forward. I needed to show up and listen to stories offered as a sacred trust by brave storytellers whose names I will never forget.

The gang members I remember most were children the churches I've worked in have failed. Sure, many success stories came from the same churches, and I remember and give thanks for every single one, but I also remember those who found identity through gang colors rather than baptism. I remember those who called when they were afraid and alone in a precinct or in the Tombs. I remember going to court and the rigors of visiting at Rikers Island. I know some who have come out and built new lives with new families and some who will spend their lives behind bars. I know their names and their stories too, and some of our stories are now forever linked.

Most Christians in the mainline can choose proximity or distance from those on the margins, and most choose the latter. But it does not have to be that way. Those who live in places of protected privilege can find ways to jump the fence, intentionally seeking to listen and learn from the stories of those under attack in these days. A congregation may have no personal knowledge of murdered transgender women but can readily find their names and stories, attach their photographs to a cardboard cross set up in the sanctuary, leaving room to add others, as will tragically be needed. The congregation can pray for these women by name in worship, light candles, read and discuss a theology book by a transgender author, and invite a transgender preacher, although not if the members will cause them to feel like a visiting oddity. The congregation can lobby for human rights for transgender persons. Attention to the building of a wall on our southern border can distract us from all the invisible walls already in place, walls we have the power to tear down.

Decades before Extell, Trump, and the Chinese played Monopoly with the properties and lives of Manhattan neighborhood residents, Trinity received notice that it would be demolished as part of Robert Moses's "urban renewal" plans. It was 1949. Many churches were in the glory days of building expansions, but here, things began to fall apart. Robert Moses was the New York state and city official whose vast array of public works projects rearranged and transformed the city's landscape. When I lived in the Bronx, I witnessed his most devastating legacy. Moses devised what he termed a "slum clearance project." He wanted to push the poor away from areas of Manhattan where he planned to build middle-class housing. In the words of Stanley Isaacs, the Manhattan Borough President at the time, "My God, they're hounding the people out like cattle. Tens of thousands of people were thrown out of their homes by Moses with very little provision for relocation." Undeterred, Moses steered the poorest of the masses into the South Bronx.

Soon afterward, he oversaw the construction of the Cross Bronx Expressway, which ripped through the area, unsettling and displacing sixty thousand more families, who had no say in the matter. I wrote about this history in my memoir about the South Bronx, but at the time, I had no idea that Moses's "slum clearance project" was initiated right in what would become my new neighborhood. The same urban-planning crusade that slashed through the Bronx razed thirty-seven acres of brownstone and tenement buildings around Trinity in the 1950s. Moses offered $5,000 for the church members to move elsewhere—suggesting the suburbs of Westchester, thereby clearing the path for him to tear down the church building and widen the street.

I loved learning about the elderly German women of the congregation who stood arm-in-arm in the street, blocking the bulldozers of the behemoth developer. I discovered these stalwart women in old photographs. Most likely, the church avoided destruction because the stubborn perseverance of the members joined forces with the political savvy of the pastor at the time, the Reverend George Saunders, who had a good friend on the Real Estate Board of New York.

The community that rose up around the church in the wake of Moses retained an intense level of diversity, with public-housing projects on one side of the street and middle-income rent-stabilized apartments on the other. The landscape is now joined by sleek high-rises that have no room for the poor and stretch the limits of middle and working classes. What did Moses hope to gain by widening West 100th Street? He wanted to put the greatest distance possible between the poor and everyone else. In such a tight urban space, physical distance is counted in feet rather than miles, but every inch comes with a dollar sign in this real estate game that leaves our nation fragmented. Anyone who cares about human community loses.

In my congregation, some enjoy privileges that others can only dream of. We don't all speak the same language or like the same music. Sometimes people get on each other's nerves. But Jesus gathers us week after week, in one basket. We learn each other's names and prayer concerns. A slab of black marble tops the altar where we gather. Traces of wax from all those votive candles still smudge the surface, a lingering memory of the names we recalled at the remembrance service, the lives brutally snuffed out. Whenever I consider scraping the wax off, I stop myself because it testifies that two sex workers, three hundred candles, and Jesus's own body and blood belong at the same table.

Ash Wednesday

6

Whiter Than Snow

> I have a great relationship with the blacks.

A former intern at Trinity, Paul Baile, who later served an unusual call with one church in Texas and one across the border in Mexico, brought up the presence of whiteness in the story of Jesus's transfiguration, a text read in many churches on the Sunday before Ash Wednesday. In the story, Jesus's clothing becomes dazzling white in a display of divine glory. Paul called attention to the whiteness in centuries of Eurocentric liturgical art and the fact that our churches traditionally use white funeral palls and baptismal garments, associating the color white with purity and holiness. He shared his thoughts on a public platform and mentioned that he might address this problematic issue in his upcoming sermon. My colleague meant to express sensitivity to race, privilege, and power as a white pastor in Mexican and Mexican American communities. The responses he received are a master class in misdirection.

> Isaac Newton built the first practical reflecting telescope and developed a theory of color based on the observation that a prism decomposes white light into the many colors of the visible spectrum . . . if you ask a scientist, white is a color—it contains the whole spectrum—and black is the absence of color. If you ask an artist—who deals in pigments rather than wavelengths—the answer is the opposite . . . I am not an artist, but I don't think white is the presence of all colors. Isn't black made when many colors are stirred together?

A fellow Lutheran pastor responded more directly: "Caucasians are not white, only albinos are white . . . I think sometimes we need to get over our 'whiteness' and join the human race. Perhaps, when Mexicans are not labeled as animals and nonwhite immigrants are not referred to as insects and diseases that invade and infest our nation. And when future Trayvon Martins can get over their blackness."

My colleague's experience was not an isolated one. Four days after Transfiguration Sunday, we come to Ash Wednesday and the recommended penitential Psalm 51, including verse 7: "Purge me with hyssop, and I shall be clean; wash me, and I shall be whiter than snow." I confess that I didn't balk at this line until I became a pastor in the South Bronx and was the only white person in the room. I'd printed the materials without careful review for an Ash Wednesday service. All of a sudden, mid-service, there it appeared, glaring in our sanctuary like a visitor in a white hood. Of course, I knew that it was written in a different time and context, but leading a Black and Latino congregation, as a white pastor, to pray that they wish they were whiter than snow was unconscionable.

A few years ago, when Ash Wednesday approached, I flagged the line and composed a post alerting fellow clergy to consider the impact of the verse in their own contexts. Soon, the responses rolled in. Some appreciated my post, but many did not. What's telling is how frequently my original point about race was obfuscated. The physics of light was not addressed; instead, the conversation shifted to snow and laundry. Granted, the psalm uses the imagery of snow and laundry, but every reader knew that I was referring to the impact of that imagery in a nation still divided by race and in a church that remains 96 percent white. It seemed that many of our churches found it easier to talk about snow and laundry:

> Compare new-fallen snow as opposed to that leftover pile slowly melting at the edge of the parking lot—it's filled with dirt, leaves, etc.

> I'm still trying to figure out how to talk to the youth in my congregation for whom snow is mostly something they see in pictures or maybe if they happen to go to Flagstaff in the winter.

> Clean snow is white–dirty snow is black, brown, yellow, red–whatever happens to be contaminating it. This is a fact, not a racial statement.

> I think this passage is an image of laundry practices. Beating clothes with a stick so that they are washed white . . . this verse is not about skin color, it's a metaphor on laundry. You want your whites to be white, and I hate it when my clergy blacks begin to be a bit gray. . . . Did you know there's a special laundry soap for darks?

> Maybe it's because I still do the laundry in my household, but I have always associated those words with the ability of bleach and stain spray to remove the yuck we got all over our clothes. . . . If you're so concerned, translate it as "De-lint me and I will be blacker than my clergy shirt."

Another person dismissed my point by explaining that white is not always preferred—think of the expression "whitewashing." Yes, "whitewashing." I thought about it. And I thought about congregants who told of bleach added to their childhood bathwater to lighten their skin. A few who addressed my comment directly stated that such words do not matter; only actions do. True, words without actions are empty, even treacherous, if we convince ourselves that we bear no responsibility beyond thoughts, prayers, and voicing concerns. But words can have a mighty impact for good or for ill on their own as well. Words can inspire or incite as they do in newscasts, rallies, and Twitter bursts.

Ash Wednesday back in the Bronx was not my first time being the only white person in the room. During seminary, I took a class in racism at the University of Pennsylvania's School of Social Work. The class consisted of African American students, one Native American student, and me. Until then, I was used to being given the benefit of the doubt, assumed to be a decent person with good intentions. In that classroom, I quickly realized how privileged and self-serving it was for me to harbor such expectations. I had to wrestle with my identity. Like Jacob struggling through the night with a strong man who left him with a dislocated hip and a limp, I found myself uncomfortably dislocated and limping off from that class, and was the better for it.

Ash Wednesday is a day to lament and confess. It reminds me of Jesus's words to remove the log from my own eye before zeroing in on the speck in my neighbor's eye. I cannot remove the log of white privilege from my eye by my own power, and so on Ash Wednesday, I mark the sign of ashes on all who come forward and I wear it myself.

I remember that I am dust and to dust I shall return. The ashes we wear appear to be a great equalizer. Persons of every age come forward, including babies in their mother's arms and toddlers in their strollers. I mark the dusty cross on dark skin and light, freckled, pimpled, and smooth, on those without homes and those who dwell in well-appointed apartments. Yes, every one of us will die, but all deaths are not equal.

On their honeymoon in 1953, my parents visited Lübeck, Germany, to see St. Mary's Church, the world's tallest Gothic cathedral built of brick. My father wanted to show my mother where he had been baptized and confirmed. Eleven years earlier, on Palm Sunday 1942, an Allied bombing raid had attacked the church in retaliation for the Nazi bombing of England's Coventry Cathedral. When my parents visited, repairs were still underway. They could look up past the soaring arches from the sanctuary and see the sky.

Among the many works of art destroyed in the firebombing was a painted frieze that wound around the four walls of the confessional chapel. It depicted a common medieval theme: the dance of death, or *Totentanz*. In the painting, death dances with representative citizens, following a strict hierarchy. Death begins with the pope and the emperor, and then moves on to the cardinal and king. He slips a bony hand in the crook of the bishop's arm, then the mayor's. Death is always in motion, leaping off the ground while the citizens of Lübeck stand stiffly resisting the inevitable: merchant, bailiff, nobleman, knight, doctor, moneylender, monk, hermit, farmer, sexton, peasant, maid, and finally, an infant in her cradle.

For those who entered St. Mary's chapel for confession before the bombing, the cityscape of Lübeck depicted in the background brought the point even closer to home. The painting includes an exhortation to lead a righteous life while time remains. It belongs to a genre of art that spread during outbreaks of the plague. In fact, a plague claimed thousands of lives in the vicinity of St. Mary's only a year after the painting was installed.

A new version of the *Totentanz* in stained glass, completed in 1956, is a point of special pride in the now-repaired St. Mary's sanctuary. The window presents a faithful vertical version of the original, with a few striking additions. Death goes through the same social ranks, but when he reaches the baby, he is forced to his knees and covers his face with his hands. The child is Christ, and to make sure we don't miss this, a golden label floats over the baby's head: DEO. The baby in the crib, swaddled in bands for burial, appears to be rising from his crib as from a tomb, hands raised in blessing.

The other departure from the original involves the representation of the cityscape. The buildings of Lübeck are there along the bottom of the window, but the city is being attacked by angry, red tongues of fire. This beautiful window draws millions of tourists each year. The original presented a sly social commentary—the pope and peasant are waiting in line for the same dance partner, signifying the equalizing nature of our mortality. But given the church's setting and history, that's a lie. The 102 panels in this stained-glass meditation about death were created within a decade of the Shoah in Germany but make no reference to the Holocaust. Not one piece of glass suggests the truth that not all deaths are equal. Not one piece suggests the lethal alliance of fascism and the church. Instead, the scene depicts Lübeck as the victim of war with no role in and no contrition for the city's complicity in millions of deaths. Streams of visitors come, take their photographs, and purchase their postcards, but receive no invitation to meditate on how they might live their lives in the wake of the Shoah's macabre choreography.

This reminds me of visitors to plantations or historic, colonial churches in the South who don't want their vacation spoiled by hearing about the horrors of slavery. Culpability across generations is a complex subject, but one that requires attention. White tourists to Natchez, Mississippi, or Williamsburg, Virginia, ought to reflect on the chain that links slavery to Jim Crow to redlining to white privilege in our own day, and Christian visitors to the Lübeck window ought to consider the long-standing history of anti-Jewish violence in the church. The Lutheran church, to be sure, has a strong cultural strain of preferential "niceness" that shies away from unpleasant subjects. And indeed, for many, church is a place to be calmed and comforted, not agitated. There's enough agitation at work, on the news and perhaps at home. And yet the church has often been a cradle for violence. Two of the citizens snatched away in Lübeck's *Totentanz* were my Jewish grandparents. My grandfather's ashes have marked my heart and mind forever.

Lent

7

Suffer the Little Children

> The beauty that's being taken out of our cities, towns and parks will greatly be missed and never able to be comparably replaced.

The children who used to shine with their blond curls from our church's stained-glass windows were all white. The disciples depicted were white. Jesus was white. In every window, every human being was white. When German immigrants proudly placed the windows in their church in 1908, all the children who sat in their presence week after week were also white, often blond-haired Germans like the people in the glass. It is good that they could see themselves illuminated in the stories, but it's wrong that others cannot.

It's tempting to let these German immigrants off the hook—*they were just reflecting their times!*—but 1908 was also the height of German colonial rule in Africa. As Trinity's walls rose in New York, concentration camps sprung up in Namibia to confine native Africans who resisted German colonial rule. Details of this bloody era include mass deportation, forced labor, starvation, food rations, and diseases like typhoid due to unsanitary living conditions. The first genocide of the twentieth century took place on Namibia's Shark Island, a prototype for what was to come. At the same time ground was broken for Trinity's construction in 1906, women prisoners on Shark Island were forced to boil the heads of dead inmates and scrape them clean. The skulls were then shipped to Germany as trophies and for study at universities seeking to identify similarities between these skulls and those of apes, as part of Nazi race "science."

I doubt that Shark Island ever entered the minds of those building this neo-Gothic structure. They likely didn't know the history of those who came before them on the land they purchased for the church. Within my first month as Trinity's pastor, Roger, the head of the property committee, gave me a tour of the building. The tour included a trip to the boiler room, where I saw the expected boiler, hot water heater, assorted floor fans, and something that surprised me. A depression carved through the concrete floor, allowing a thin flow of water to pass under the building. Roger explained that this was the residue of a subterranean stream that once ran through Manhattan Valley and now surfaces under many buildings in the area.

This watery remnant of the past, flowing directly under what would become my office, made me curious to learn more. Fortunately, the church stands next to a library with a significant local history section curated by neighborhood history buffs. I discovered that for three hundred years, the indigenous Lenape people hunted bears, mountain lions, and deer in the native forest that once thrived on land where real estate developers now hunt down properties to devour. Long before the bright lights of Hamilton, these Lenape established the length of

Broadway as a hunting trail, extending through the forests of upstate New York and into Canada. They called it *Wickquasgeck*.

The first real estate speculators were Dutch colonists who forced the Lenape off their land in the early 1600s, pushing them west, eventually to Oklahoma. In 1626, when the Dutch supposedly "bought" *Mannahatta* from the Lenape, they built a wall around New Amsterdam to keep the Lenape out, and then the British. Today, that wall has been replaced by Wall Street, where a billion-dollar revenue stream flows from keeping human beings, adults and children, behind walls and fences in facilities run by the private prison and detention industry.

The original wall could not keep out the English. When they settled the land around Trinity, they continued Dutch efforts to turn thick woods into tillable farmland and country estates. The busy, crowded neighborhood surrounding the church today was once a bucolic escape from urban life named Bloomingdale, after a Dutch tulip-growing region. Of course, many found it far from idyllic. By 1700, the cash crop throughout the area was tobacco, farmed by enslaved Africans who made up 20 percent of New York's colonial population until emancipation came to the state in 1827. Broadway, one block from the church, changed from *Wickquasgeck* to *Brede weg* under the Dutch. It became the roadway known as Broadway when they needed it to transport bales of tobacco to the city's southern port.

The German immigrants who built Trinity arrived near the end of the 1800s as urbanization sped north from the tip of Manhattan. The next century brought Jewish refugees escaping Europe, along with Dominicans, Puerto Ricans, Haitians, Ukrainians, and others. The sanctuary that these refugees found and the land where they began to build new lives came at a cost often ignored: the many forgotten people displaced and enslaved. The subterranean stream that runs through a fissure in the foundation witnessed this history and carries our past into our present, confronting me whenever I venture down into the boiler room.

I understand that the German immigrants who arrived here and founded the church had their own struggles: they needed a place to build their own lives, and to see their own faces reflected in the sanctuary windows. But no amount of contextual explanation can undo the damaging visceral impact for nonwhite children of being surrounded by biblical scenes in which everyone, including Jesus, is white. What do those windows mean for the eight-year-old girl ready to jump from the top of a playground slide because a group of classmates derided her as an ugly, black monkey? What empowering story might she more easily believe if she had gazed up at Black Jesus in the windows? Or Black children sitting at Jesus's feet? What dangerous message do impressionable white children accept when they see the light shining only on themselves?

The Washington National Cathedral has removed stained-glass windows honoring confederate generals Robert E. Lee and Stonewall Jackson. In one of Yale University's dining halls, an African American dishwasher used a broomstick to dislodge and smash a stained-glass window that depicted two slaves standing in a field with bales of cotton balanced on their heads. "I shouldn't have to come to work and see things like that," he said. What about coming to church and seeing nothing but a white Jesus? Is the answer to remove them all and lose what many consider priceless art? What about the priceless life of a little girl on top of a slide? I must admit to my own cowardly relief in having that decision taken out of my hands.

Soon after I arrived as a new pastor at the church, our stained glass had to be removed, disassembled, and replaced by clear plexiglass because of the jackhammers breaking into bedrock under the lot beside us for new luxury apartments. I watched as immigrants from Mexico and Eastern Europe donned surgical masks and gloves to gently handle this fragile body of art made by German immigrants a century ago. The task required a five-man relay. The first in the relay climbed up and pried each section of glass from its wooden frame. The next received it on the outside and lowered it to a waiting partner, who handed it off to a fourth. The fourth carried it to a makeshift wooden table. There, the final man in the relay examined each piece as if for an autopsy, scrupulously cataloging weaknesses, defects, and damages. I watched them swath the glass in gauzy wrappings, nail them inside wooden boxes, and load them for burial in a dark rental unit at Manhattan Mini-Storage.

All of this was done as preparation for some possible future rebirth. Personally, I doubt the windows will see the light of day again due to the prohibitive cost of re-leading and re-installation, over half a million dollars, and I think it is all for the best. Is it unfair to equate the windows of our churches to the confederate statues that Trump called, "beauty that [would] greatly be missed and never able to be comparably replaced"? Many will recoil at the comparison, but I think it merits reflection. White Jesus no longer shines through our windows, but white privilege is not so easily dismantled, and the decision of what to do with our inherited visual representations is not usually settled with such ease.

A clergy colleague recently told me about a job interview in which she asked the church call committee what she might do as their pastor that would be beyond the pale. They told her that it would be to remove the very large painting directly above the altar, a depiction of white Jesus in prayer in the garden of Gethsemane. Undoubtedly, that sacred painting has absorbed the anxieties, losses, fears, and tears of many who've sat in that church's pews and lifted up their prayers. My friend was called as their pastor, and when I attended her ordination, I noticed an equally large wall space on either side of the painting of white Jesus. Sometimes, instead of subtracting, we can add and create ongoing history.

In my first weeks at Trinity before the windows came down, we hung a huge tapestry from our organ loft called "The Tree of Life" by the Haitian artist Jacques-Richard Chéry. The work centers on a tree loaded with ripe fruits recognizable throughout the Caribbean. A Black Jesus hangs from the tree, wounded, but very much alive. I was surprised to enter the sanctuary one afternoon and find the tapestry missing. I eventually located it folded up in the organ loft. It turns out that an organist who rented the space for a concert had removed it because "it might offend the concert guests."

A while back, I received a Facebook message from a colleague on the other side of the country. He wrote from Los Angeles to tell me about a young woman he'd known through campus ministry who now lived in Brooklyn with her husband and their two young sons. The family had not yet connected to an East Coast church community when they reached out to my colleague from the shadowlands of trauma, and he quickly messaged me. Although they lived in Brooklyn, this couple was spending almost all their time in the pediatric intensive care unit of a Manhattan hospital where their fifteen-month-old son lay dying.

I was in another hospital when the message came, having just emerged from surgery with a new hip. It would take a few weeks before I could venture out. Fortunately, my seminary intern, Gretchen, rose to the task, though she described herself as halting and unsteady before the door of the intensive care unit. Her ministry was all the better for it as she stumbled with this family on ground where no one can go with sure feet. Gretchen was young and inexperienced for a task like this, but I can attest that experience does nothing to make such a journey any easier.

Gretchen helped Charlie, the five-year-old big brother, say goodbye. She stayed beside his parents as they quavered on the edge of impossible decisions. I recovered in time to attend the funeral. Charlie clung to his mother, serious and sad. His baby brother laughed from the huge photos prepared by coworkers in his father's design company, doing what they knew how to do. Gretchen preached and I led prayers around a small white coffin tenderly covered with favorite stuffed animals.

For many Sundays afterward, Charlie hid behind his parents' legs. He rarely spoke. He didn't want to attend Sunday School. Instead, he sat with his dad and drew pictures of cars and rockets, like the ones on the funeral bulletin beside the prayer he spoke four days before his brother's death: "Dear God, please send us a rocket ship so Jakey and me can go to the stars. I love Jakey. Amen." Then one Sunday, Charlie decided to join the other children in Sunday School with his father nearby. Another young seminarian had prepared a lesson on Tabitha for that day. She told the children the story of Tabitha's death, of the widows who mourned and cherished the woven tunics Tabitha had made them, and then of Peter raising her from her deathbed. The teacher suddenly realized her "error." Wouldn't Charlie wonder why

Jesus did not bring his brother back to life? Why hadn't God answered his prayers and those of his parents? And then this quiet little boy, for the first time ever in class, began to speak. He told his classmates that his brother had died and was with Jesus in heaven. He showed them the woven bracelet he wore to remind him of his brother, the same way the widows showed Peter their woven tunics. The class, including children with ADHD who get a break from their meds on the weekends, sat perfectly still. Every eye and every ear focused on the brave testimony of their classmate who had walked in the valley of the shadow of death and was speaking about it.

Then Paradise stood up, named in defiance of all the statistics against her as a young, Black girl. Her grandmother had seen to her braids clasped with glittering butterflies in every color of the rainbow. Her grandmother sees to everything good in her life. Now, Paradise pushed back her chair to stand and give her classmate a hug. As she leaned over, her bedazzled black braids fell around his blond head. Following her lead, one by one, every child rose and hugged Charlie, and then, his father.

I have no illusions that such feel-good, personal moments dismantle the racist structures that emerge between our children or lessen the distance between their experiences and the kinds of injustices they face. Charlie is wounded by a terrible loss, but will enjoy privileges Paradise will never know. Superficial diversity is dangerous because it can create a sense of progress that isn't real. It can prevent us from admitting how bad things are and feeling convicted to change them. Yet, as part of change, I do believe that multiplying moments of shared experience and closeness matters, not to be touted as a boast of achievement, but as a reminder of how much is at stake and how much is possible.

The moment passed and the children sat back down to weave paper place mats for the upcoming Thanksgiving dinner. The children's brightly colored strips of paper woven in and out will decorate tables the following Thursday, where nearly a thousand hungry people will gather for a meal, thanks to many volunteers, including a large group from a neighboring synagogue. When Thursday arrived, Paradise's grandmother brought her brood of three to the meal. Paradise noticed the place mats instantly and proudly pointed out her work. Her grandmother told me this at our Wednesday morning prayer group. She arrived early for the meeting, and before she even sat down, I noticed her tears and ran to get the box of tissues. She needed surgery for gallstones and was worried about the children. Could she trust her daughter to get them to and from school? She told me about another daughter born with full-blown AIDS in the eighties. Experimental AZT gave her two years instead of the predicted six months, but she died in December and the anniversary was coming up.

Others arrived for the prayer meeting. Before we prayed, we read a text from the upcoming Sunday. "A shoot shall come out from the stump of Jesse. . . . The spirit of the Lord shall rest on him, the spirit of wisdom and understanding, the spirit of counsel and might" (Isa. 11:2). The grandmother interrupted. "That sounds familiar!" she said. It should; I spoke those words when Paradise and her little brothers were baptized, as I placed my hands on each of their promise-drenched heads.

Banging noises from our boiler room punctuated our prayers. We could hear the chimney sweeps breaking into the side of an underground chimney that had not been cleaned in a century. The distraction was necessary. The cleaning needed doing, or the youth who slept in our shelter, and my family who slept in the parsonage attached to the church, might slumber into carbon-monoxide-induced oblivion.

With aging churches, the repair work never ends. There is much to dismantle and much to rebuild. Some days, it worries me and wears me down, but not enough to stop me. To make matters worse, our architect quit, forcing us to start over again with a new architect and new drawings. The latest architectural plans are spread out on my desk. On top of them rests a letter written by a nine-year-old girl. Her mother made her write it for speaking out of turn in church. "Dear Pastor Heidi, I am sorry for disrespecting the reading to God and I won't do it again." The apology is sweet, but what I love is the picture she drew underneath: a brown-skinned girl with a sparkly flower on her chest smiles widely inside the outline of a heart. The girl's arms are raised to hold high a green arc, which looks like a jump rope. The word "God" is written beside the drawing with an arrow pointing straight at the girl. When God is a smiling, brown-skinned girl with a sparkly flower on her chest, we see that despite ourselves, Jesus will not be denied or deterred from blessing the children: for it is to such as these that the kin-dom of God belongs (see Luke 18:16).

8

Leap before You Look

This is about safety. It has nothing to do with religion.

As a mother, I can't understand how anyone can abandon her children to the streets. When our two children lived at home with us, I never could fall asleep until I knew they were safely home. It's one advantage of a creaky, old house. Even from our bedroom on the third floor, I could hear the slightest sound of Ana or Hans coming into the house after a late night out with friends. Only then could I relax. How can a mother lock her child out? How can a mother tell her child she wishes they had never been born? How can a parent turn a cold ear to a child's brokenhearted cry?

Carlos grew up in the Southwest with a homophobic, fundamentalist Christian family who told him to "stop acting like a girl and be a man." Verbally abused throughout his childhood and early adolescence by his parents, Carlos still hurts over his father's parting shot: "You're going to New York City and get AIDS and be a faggot and die." As news of the Pulse Nightclub massacre broke, I only wished to spare the youth in our shelter the trauma of hearing about it, but of course, they heard. In his distress, Carlos reached out with hope against hope and called his mother, who coldly told him that it was "God's retribution." One version or another of this story has been repeated over six hundred times since we opened Trinity Place Shelter.

When Hurricane Sandy approached the city, we stocked up on water, flashlights, batteries, and extra food. Derrick excitedly told our staff that his grandmother had invited him to stay in her home with his siblings because she felt that the family should be together during the storm. Derrick was thrilled that she included him. It was going to be his first family event since his abusive father kicked him out in the middle of high school for being gay. According to Derrick, his father was away and so he would be safe.

Everyone else hunkered down at the shelter and enjoyed board games, movies, music, and extra snacks while winds and rain pounded outside. I went to bed and our social worker Wendy settled in for the night. At eleven o'clock, when the whole city was shut down by the storm, Wendy got a phone call from Derrick. His father had shown up at the grandmother's house in the Bronx, beaten him, and thrown him outside in the middle of the hurricane. Wendy told him we'd pay for the car service to pick him up. When Derrick arrived, soaked and shaking, Wendy ushered him in and paid the driver. Derrick stepped inside and said with relief, "I'm so glad to be home!"

On a different night, Kimmy came in and said: "Now it's my time to feel human, my three hours to feel human," referring to the hours before she falls asleep. Another resident put it like this:

> I don't feel like I live in a shelter—I live in a home. . . . You can let your guard down here in a way that you absolutely can't do anywhere else. I feel more at home here, more home here, than I have anywhere

> else. Even when I had my own place, renting a room from some cis-straight guy, I didn't feel I had the freedom to be myself in the way I do here. We get a lot of freedom here which is part of why people feel so comfortable here. For example, we have a great kitchen where we can cook our own food that's bought for us. We can also shower anytime we want, even in the middle of the night. Things like that make us feel more in control and still free. Laughter is the sound you hear the most at Trinity Place, not fighting or yelling.

This is a splendid testimonial for Trinity Place, but under these grand words run deep sadness and trauma, because parental love is absent, because one's home of origin is no longer safe, or never was.

Trump's statement about safety came in the wake of his Muslim ban, despite the fact that many more citizens have been killed by white men with no connection to Islam than by Muslim terrorists or foreigners. His ban does have to do with religion though, a religion that condemns Muslims to hell in an afterlife that may as well begin now. This belief system teaches its disciples to deeply fear the thought of demographic "replacement." "Christian values" include bathrooms safe from transgender people, keeping marriage safely heterosexual, and an ethical duty to protect daughters from brown-skinned "animals" in the streets who might attack or even enter their beds. In the name of "safety," many people are becoming less safe.

The church has a long history of offering safe spaces, or sanctuary, going back thousands of years. God instructed the Hebrews freed from slavery to establish "cities of refuge" where "anyone who kills a person without intent or by mistake may flee there; they shall be for you a refuge from the avenger of blood. . . . And if the avenger of blood is in pursuit, they shall not give up the slayer" (Josh. 20:3, 5). A person could remain in the sanctuary city until it was safe for them to leave.

Sanctuary cities have been in the news lately: The president often threatens to punish them. A sanctuary city like New York has local laws that aim to protect undocumented immigrants from deportation or prosecution, despite federal immigration law. In a sanctuary city, a person should be able to seek emergency medical care without fear of the hospital's alerting immigration authorities. Apart from expressing compassion, this helps keep everybody safer from communicable diseases.

Churches also have a history of providing physical sanctuary to refugees and asylum-seekers; and churches often have sanctuaries, or holy spaces set aside for worship, though any space of prayer can be a sanctuary. Ironically, providing sanctuary demands taking risks and putting our own safety, real or imagined, on the line. My own denomination voted to become a Sanctuary Church in a national assembly held in the summer of 2019. What that means is wide-ranging, but it does include a commitment to provide physical sanctuary when needed. Trinity houses residents who seek sanctuary because of their sexual orientation or gender identity, refugees from hate, including some from other countries seeking asylum: a young, gay man from Honduras, a transgender woman from Jamaica, and another from Mexico, all fleeing for their lives.

It was the last Sunday of June in 2004, the day of New York City's Pride parade. I sat drinking my early morning coffee—part of an introvert routine that includes prayer, breakfast, and a few non-challenging pieces in the *Sunday Times* (Vows, Modern Love)—when I saw the headline: "For Young Gays on the Streets, Survival Comes before Pride; Few Beds for Growing Class of Homeless." The article noted that as mainstream media becomes more LGBTQIA+ friendly, more youth come out to their families, only to find themselves rejected, often kicked to the street, "a growing legion of the disowned and the dispossessed, most of them Black and Latino, an increasing number of them H.I.V. positive and still in the throes of adolescence." What really shocked me was the detail that in a city of over eight million people, there were only a few dozen beds available for this particular homeless population of nearly ten thousand. Other shelters were often unsafe, with queer young people bullied by staff and even urinated on as they slept. I thought of my own adolescent children safe in their beds and my heart seized. On the other hand, what could I do? What could we do?

I had my sermon planned, but now I felt compelled to share what I'd learned about the plight of homeless queer youth. The response I received after worship told me that I was not the only one who longed to take action. Recognizing that churches had created much of this problem, Trinity wanted to be part of the solution, but it didn't seem realistic. Our century-old building desperately needed repairs. We had a daunting budgetary deficit. What could we possibly do?

The following year, a call went out for faith communities to open their doors for one week during some of the coldest nights of winter, accommodating the overflow from the few existing shelters. This opportunity fit our limited resources. Our intern, Chris Wogaman, eagerly coordinated the effort, having once experienced homelessness as a young gay man in the city. At some point during our first week of providing shelter, which stretched into three, we began to imagine doing more. We could not count on a better-resourced congregation to care for these homeless youth. When the call went out to religious institutions throughout the city to open their doors for one week, only three churches responded positively. Based on the others I spoke with, most deemed it too much of a risk. In some cases, the church-approval process had so many layers and was so lengthy that by the time the decision-makers had calculated all the risks and arrived at their decision, the winter crisis would have passed.

Opening Trinity Place was not a controversial issue for the majority of my congregation, whose concerns mostly revolved around the practical, like space sharing and finances. Kevin Lotz, our vice president and a social worker, mitigated any further anxieties when he presented an extremely thorough plan and assumed the role of shelter director. I did worry, however, about the response from our newer, immigrant members who had been raised in a more conservative church culture. When we had a meeting to discuss the proposal after our Spanish worship service one Sunday, it was clear that nobody wanted to be branded as prejudiced. People veiled their concerns by saying things like, "I am not personally opposed to this, but I bet my friends and family might be, and thus the shelter might impede our desired outreach and growth." I listened with a sinking heart.

I wanted to mention Mexico's rich history among its indigenous cultures of accepting varied sexual orientations and what today might be considered as genderqueer persons going back to pre-Columbian times, when cross-dressing Aztecs led worship and people celebrated Mayan gods who belie the colonial gender binary. It seemed to me that homophobia and transphobia arrived along with the Spanish conquistadores. But before I could gear up to speak, Juana stood up: "You know, in other churches, everyone is separate. There is a mass in one language and a mass in another language and people don't even talk to each other. Here we are welcomed and the church wants to worship together." We had provided Juana's first experience of regular bilingual worship, something she now treasured.

When Juana's father died, her grief was intensified. Being undocumented meant that she could not return to Mexico for the funeral. She asked if we could have our own memorial service, even though, as she said sadly, hardly anyone would attend since nobody here knew him. At her insisting, we made only a handful of bulletins. We quickly made more on the day of the service, when the pews began filling beyond expectations. I led the worship in Spanish, but many of the people attending spoke only English. Their presence was poignantly eloquent.

At our meeting for the shelter proposal, Juana concluded: "I used to be uncomfortable around gay people. But here my mind has changed. People are people and everyone deserves to be treated with respect and love. We know what it's like to be unwanted but here we have been welcomed, so we should welcome these rejected young people with nowhere else to go." It turned out that the pastor didn't need to give a hectoring history lesson. The vote in favor of the shelter was unanimous. On June 12, 2006, Trinity Place Shelter opened and served its first dinner to the youth: a feast of tortillas, salad, rice, and chicken *mole* lovingly prepared by the Mexican church mothers.

Sometime later, I was sitting with Alleyna at a table in the church basement eating lasagna. "So," she asked me, "when are you going to give me the lecture?" The lecture? I had no idea what Alleyna meant. "The one that every minister gives me," she clarified. "What lecture is that?" I asked. "The one where you tell me I'm going to hell." Alleyna had only been staying at the shelter for a few weeks, but she stood out for her positive attitude. When dishes needed washing or the floor needed sweeping, most residents bickered over whose turn it was to do which chore, or questioned who left the cereal bowl on the table and who left the wet towel on the floor. Alleyna simply picked up the broom or headed for the kitchen sink and went to work. Every morning when I looked in to say hello and see how things were going, a time of day when most are sullen with sleep, Alleyna offered a friendly greeting, but now she told me with some somberness: "The reason they say I'm going to hell is that I worship the devil."

Alleyna did not fit my vision of a devil-worshipper. While some might find her appearance off-putting—charcoal circles around her eyes, blackened lips, and spiked dog collars around her neck and wrists that matched her pointed facial piercings—her kindness shone through the makeup. I did not believe this self-confessed devil-worshipper was what she claimed to be. So I asked her to tell me what she meant about worshipping the devil, and then I listened.

Alleyna told me that she could not believe that God ruled the world. Her reasoning was simple: How could God be in control with so many terrible things going on? How could a loving God allow all the damage that had been done to her? She also said that she had to look out for herself because she couldn't count on anyone else. Some pious people had once informed her that she was idolatrously worshipping herself—or, she added, the devil. Did Alleyna participate in any demonic rites, any satanic ceremonies? No. Did she believe in hurting other people? "Of course not!" she said, looking horrified. If Alleyna's questions about God pave the road to hell, she will have plenty of saintly company. The burden weighs on others to show her that real, trustworthy love exists and that people exist whom she can count on to provide support and to appreciate her for who she is. Someone asked if there was any parmesan cheese for the lasagna, and Alleyna jumped up to get it. I thought of the Jewish saying that claims thousands of angels go before every human being, crying, "Make way, make way, for the image of God."

In some ways, church history was repeating itself. Trinity began in a storefront but lost the space when the congregant who owned the store declared bankruptcy. The firehouse just down the street, complete with a stable full of horses used to pull the heavy wagons, turned out to be a godsend for the small church. Local merchants were loath to expose their freshly butchered meat, baked goods, and produce to the swarms of flies attracted by the horses. Those disgusting horse flies drove away most business and enabled Trinity to lease an empty storefront across from the firehouse at a good price, forty-eight dollars a month.

Unfortunately, with low attendance, long meetings, and flies, the pastor left for Connecticut within nine months, citing a decline in health due to "excessive exertion." Despite his frustration and failing stamina, Pastor Tappert took a bold initiative during his brief stay, which he described in his journal:

> Since there was no public school in this whole district and children roamed the streets at all hours, we started a school there. The school was well attended from the start. A man, who was our organist, was engaged as a teacher. A woman, trained as a school teacher, and two

> girls with training in kindergarten instruction were also employed. Soon all the space at our disposal was filled.

Even before having a proper building, the church provided a sanctuary in its storefront for neighborhood youth who "roamed the streets." Now, youth forced to roam from every state and around the world come to fill the modest space at our disposal. At this point, nearly six hundred youth have found a sanctuary when they needed it because the church is willing to take a risk.

Many of the seminary students I have supervised for internship in both the Bronx and Manhattan came to us wanting to learn in a more diverse context than they'd previously known. They demonstrated a willingness to be dislocated for the sake of their vocation. My own life changed one evening during seminary when I decided to put off writing a paper and attend a lecture instead. I based that life-changing decision mostly on the impulse to procrastinate—and also on the wine and cheese that I knew would be available at the lecture. The speaker, Bishop Juan Čobrda, served in Argentina during the "Dirty War" that brought terror to the country from 1976 until 1983. During that time, a military junta had seized control of the government and waged a campaign against anyone allegedly affiliated with communism. Labor unions, artists, intellectuals, university students, and professors were all targeted. Dissidents and innocent civilians alike were arrested and vanished without a trace—a total of thirty thousand *desaparecidos*, or "disappeared." People of faith, both Christians and Jews, courageously tried to advocate for and rescue the disappearing people, and some paid for their efforts with their lives.

Bishop Čobrda had seen many of his friends and colleagues vanish. His own brother was imprisoned and tortured. The government learned about Čobrda's work in advocating for thousands of refugees and labeled him as a subversive element. Because he had a target on his back, he eventually decided to take his family and settle in the US in exile. I sat captivated as Bishop Čobrda spoke with passion about faith in the face of tyranny. He stood among us as a fierce steward of the mysteries of God and I longed to know more.

After the lecture, I approached him with a stuttering attempt at thanks, and he immediately told me that I should go to Argentina. What? He had just left because of the danger and now he suggested that I should go there? Yes. I should go that I might experience firsthand the courage of the church. My first thought was, *Um, how could I do that?* He told me to apply for a scholarship from Lutheran World Federation and go to seminary in Buenos Aires.

A year later, I transferred to ISEDET (Instituto Superior de Estudios Teológicos), an ecumenical, Protestant seminary in Buenos Aires. At the same time that I first met Bishop Čobrda, ISEDET was planning a meeting focused on youth and human rights. In retaliation, the government firebombed the library, destroying two thousand books. By the time I enrolled, the library had been repaired, but the seminary remained in the junta's sites, with student names and files kept by the government.

My time in Argentina ended after fifteen months, when I returned one night to the small home I shared in the squatters' area with my housemates, two young Argentine women active in human rights work. All of our possessions were strewn around the house. Neighbors told us that military police had searched our home. I'm still not sure what they were looking for, but I realized that my presence as a foreigner was drawing attention and increased risk, not only to myself, but also to the women I lived with. It was time for me to return home anyway, as I felt called to ministry in my own country.

I never imagined the increasing fascist parallels that would surface here in the United States. I remember control of the media under the dictatorship in Argentina. Of course, the state ruled its own airwaves and print material, but a small number of English-language magazines, such as *Time* and *Newsweek* and several international newspapers, were available in Buenos Aires. If you flipped through any of these publications, you'd invariably notice sections missing. Items that the government did not want its people to read had been cut out by hand. I used to wonder who was sitting around in a room with scissors doing this shameless work. Now the scissors are electronic, and disastrously more efficient.

The nature of taking a risk is the inability to anticipate the unknowns ahead. That was true in Argentina and it is true in our church basement. A seminarian doing her fieldwork at our church arrived early one morning to prepare for the children's Sunday School. While setting out Bibles and art supplies, she noticed a balled-up paper towel on one of the tables. She grabbed it to throw away and felt something sharp. The needle inside the crumpled paper had pricked her and her hand was bleeding.

A doctor in my congregation told me that getting stuck accidentally with a needle can be deeply traumatic for first-year hospital interns. The anxiety level after these incidents is usually much higher than the likelihood of any serious infection. The doctor believes this is because it's often the first time that young residents are goaded into facing their own mortality. While this might be expected in the day-to-day duties of medical students in training, it's not something one anticipates while setting up for Sunday School.

Ronee, a resident in our shelter, has been diabetic since childhood and needs to inject herself with insulin four times a day. We have sharps containers at the shelter, but when this young woman was out during the day, she had been wrapping her used needles in paper towels and stuffing them into her backpack. At some point, when Ronee was getting ready to leave the shelter for the day, the wrapped needle fell out of her backpack onto the table next to her bed. In the morning, when the beds were rolled away, the social worker in charge scanned the room but didn't see the needle.

Our seminarian went to the emergency room. I carefully put the needle in my office because I wanted to show the social worker that it was a needle for insulin and not for illicit drugs. I should have just taken a photo of it with my phone and put it in the sharps container. Instead, when I brought the towel and needle into the shelter office that night, I pricked myself with the same dirty needle.

Although Ronee had tested negative for HIV, she was considered high risk. Now both the seminarian and I were on the post-exposure-prophylaxis HIV regimen, even though it was extremely unlikely that we'd been exposed to anything. The informative paperwork that came with my pills was sealed in blue tape to ensure privacy, as though I had a dirty little secret to hide. When it comes to HIV, even taking precautions makes one suspect. The highlighted instructions stuck on the bottles refer to "your infection" as though it's a given. I was advised not to breastfeed.

Twice a day, I felt a sudden solidarity with my friends and acquaintances who take daily HIV medications as a matter of course. Every morning and evening, I felt grateful for the existence of these meds and the improvements that have been made to lower their level of toxicity and reduce side effects. I felt grateful for the years of rich life these pills make possible and thankful for the courage and perseverance of those who endured years of a regimen that was far more taxing. And twice a day, as I paused to swallow, I also paused to pray for the many people around the world who can't access a life-saving medication that costs around $2500 a month without insurance. I thought of the stigma that still surrounds the virus.

I remember the early '80s and the many funerals I led for young mothers who died of AIDS in the South Bronx. My present congregation has a garden behind the church with roses, peonies, ferns, and a fig tree where ashes of some early AIDS victims are buried. Funeral homes did not want to touch their bodies and some cemeteries didn't want their remains. That was thirty-some years ago, but the taint persists. When a young man in our shelter tested positive, he reacted by wanting to kill himself. He feared being sick, but he also dreaded being a pariah among his peers.

This entire incident is not what one expects in the church fellowship hall, but that's the only space we have. We set out tables where homeless youth can enjoy spaghetti and meatballs at night and children can delight in Bible drama and art projects the next morning. Yet because some of the young people inject hormones (long needles) or insulin (short needles), no precautions are foolproof. We've fine-tuned our protocols to be as fail-safe as possible, but we can only stay perfectly secure by staying away or closing the doors to this population.

That is not an option for us because our call draws us close to the sharp edges of life. We serve a call that exposes our vulnerabilities as we refuse to stand apart from the pain and need around us. Our call puts us all at risk. As Paul told the Corinthians: "For while we live, we are always being given up to death for Jesus' sake, so that the life of Jesus may be made visible in our mortal flesh. So death is at work in us, but life in you" (2 Cor. 4:11–12).

The president is right that concern for safety is not about religion, at least not a religion of following Jesus, which is always a close call. In December of 1940, less than a month after the bombing of Coventry Cathedral, W. H. Auden wrote "Leap before You Look," a poem about the need to leap into the unknown, lest the quest for safety become a paralyzing dream. Auden's charge remains timely. Churches and church leaders who avoid risk-taking in order to feel more secure instead risk losing what matters most.

9

Measuring Up

Hello Miss Piggy, Hello Miss Housekeeping.

Every morning, our shelter residents roll their beds away, a chore they have named "bed Tetris," due to the challenge of fitting all ten beds into a very small space. They shower, eat breakfast, put on makeup and fix their hair, if that's their choice, and hurry out the door for school or internships or jobs. One morning a week, after all of this activity, our basement transitions into a protected space for immigrant workers to discuss labor violations with lawyers and organizers.

Some food-service workers attend our church. Other church members have the resources to frequent nearby restaurants and now choose to boycott the ones that treat their workers unjustly and to prod the owners to embrace ethical labor practices. The Indus Valley Indian restaurant, a block away from the church, was one of my neighborhood favorites. A typical Yelp review nails it: "This place is so GOOD. Great service! Great food! Great ambiance! Will be back!" Unfortunately, we won't be back until the owners stop stealing workers' wages. Those servers ride around on their bikes delivering hot chicken tikka masala, spicy lamb vindaloo, nan, and so much more, for three dollars an hour. While it's true that they receive tips for delivery, owners require their servers to do indoor work for the restaurant—sweeping up, hosing down, and receiving and stocking the many items that arrive—all for the same three dollars an hour, often while enduring verbal abuse.

Those who dared to complain were fired. They won a court case for $700,000 in back wages, but have not been able to collect anything. In a successful attempt to evade judgment, the name of the restaurant was changed from Indus Valley to Manhattan Valley. A close friend of the real owners was put in charge. According to some of the workers, there are two computers in use, one for credit card charges and one for cash. The owner has been seen filling takeout containers with cash, covering it with food, and removing it from the premises. This happens throughout the city.

Cai Shuang Chen came from China anticipating better labor laws and conditions. Instead, he ended up working twelve-hour days, seven days a week, for less than four dollars an hour. A judge awarded him $327,738 in stolen wages but, like the Mexican delivery workers in our neighborhood, he cannot access the money because the restaurant he worked for no longer exists. In reality, it's operating just fine under a new name. The restaurant owners can do this legally. Efforts to raise the minimum wage do nothing where labor laws are not enforced or fall prey to loopholes, and the New York State Department of Labor has a backlog of sixteen thousand cases.

Picketing these businesses can make a difference. Trinity joined with churches, synagogues, student groups, and other neighbors in a Justice Will Be Served! Campaign that included canvassing businesses, asking owners to sign an agreement to follow labor laws, and boycotting and picketing restaurants that refused to comply. We always held our press conferences in three languages—English, Spanish, and Mandarin—so representative workers could speak. We had some success. After one restaurant lost so many customers that it had to close, the owner of another one under threat of boycott called in his workers to negotiate a plan for just pay, including back wages.

These were smallish, local businesses, but we also heard workers from a commercial giant, Domino's Pizza. Carlos Herrera, from Mexico, often worked sixty-five hours a week as a deliveryman for Domino's but was paid for just forty-five hours. Anatole Yameogo, from Burkina Faso, worked from 10:00 a.m. to 8:00 p.m. one Saturday, yet his pay stub noted only five hours that day. Both complained and Carlos was fired, but they took the uncommon step of filing a lawsuit against Domino's along with dozens of other bicycle deliverymen who carry pizzas around the city. When these workers asked me to stand with them and speak out with them, I did. I knew we were on to something when I got a letter from the Domino's headquarters threatening to sue me and another local pastor if we continued to voice our public support of a boycott. It was worth it. The workers won a $1.3 million dollar settlement from Domino's for sixty-three deliverymen who received between $61,000 and $400 each.

Despite the efforts of the Hospitality Alliance, a restaurant lobby, to kill it, the SWEAT bill passed in Albany. But lobbyists are still pressuring the governor not to sign it. As of this date, he has not. Before the passage of the bill, I received emails, letters, and a call from one of the workers urging me to attend a press conference in Albany in support of the bill. Unfortunately, I had other church obligations that prevented me from attending, a recurrent dilemma. So many important things vie for attention. How do we decide where to focus our efforts?

Some believe that community organizing, or labor organizing work, stands at odds with the true mission of the church. The pastor belongs at the altar and, at best, the laity belong on the picket lines, although many would object to that as well. I have long struggled with the gospel story of sisters Mary and Martha. Jesus's intimacy with this particular family fascinates me. The sisters live together without husbands or children. Their brother Lazarus lives with them too, but not as the head of household or homeowner. Jesus chose this home as a place of respite and refuge, despite the fact that it challenges traditional family values and gender expectations of the time—or maybe because of that.

In the story, Mary assumes the position of a disciple learning at Jesus's feet, doing what only men were allowed to do in her time. Based on one set of the comments I received after my *Good Morning America* appearance, the first-century stigma lingers still:

> I don't listen to women who call themselves pastor. Nor the churches who employ them. . . . This so- called "Pastor" is a political operative and a liar, not a person of the cloth. . . . How many rocks did ABC have to turn over to find this "pastor"? And how do we know it isn't just another one of Hollywood's actors, playing make-believe? . . . Women are simply bad at Revrending. Maybe, like wrestling, a trannie Revrend could naturally be better at it for some reason? Honestly. Idk . . . Some ugly slag-ass girl-preacher wails some lefty garbage and this is news? When did Ozzy Osborn become a pastor? . . . She looks EXTREMELY liberal. My spider bias sense is tingling. I'm sure Streptococcus cherry picked her for this interview. I'll say this, it looks like she wouldn't be any threat to the choir or alter boys, you might want

> to watch her around the choirgirls though. . . . What church does she pastor? Is it the church of the "Fat, ugly lesbians'? . . . I think "Heidi" was originally Henry. . . . Looks like a guy in drag. Wouldn't surprise me. . . . Tell us about being nothing more than a bag of meat.

Why would someone feel uncomfortable spouting this after their president publicly called the Venezuelan Miss Universe "Miss Piggy" after she gained some weight and then, after complaints about that, "Miss Housekeeping"? The first century may have been kinder. We often talk about intersectionality on the left, but here we see it on the right. My comments on the show focused only on immigration. Over a difference of opinion, the writers identified me as the worst things they can imagine: a lesbian, ugly, a potential sexual predator, and most interestingly, a man. I suppose that according to this worldview, a transgender woman is the worst of all since they remain a male gender-betrayer.

Jesus, on the other hand, affirms Mary's gender-bending position as a disciple pondering his words. Martha appears to be shouldering more traditional woman's work, preparing the meal to set before Jesus. Martha complains about her sister just sitting there while she runs around doing all the work. It's an unfair division of labor. Jesus's response seems harsh: "Martha, Martha, you are worried and distracted by many things; there is need of only one thing. Mary has chosen the better part, which will not be taken away from her" (Luke 10:41–42).

This story appears in Luke's Gospel. Luke also writes in the book of Acts about two forms of ministry: deacons who distribute food to those in need and serve at the table, and the preachers and teachers of God's word. Some scholars believe that Luke's story of Martha and Mary affirms that women are called to both of these ministries, what Elisabeth Schüssler Fiorenza calls a discipleship of equals in the early church.

A "discipleship of equals" has a nice ring to it, but Martha and Mary are usually pitted against one another. Rigid binaries abound: work/prayer, contemplation/action, spiritual/worldly, inward/outward. The theologian Paul Tillich preached one of his most famous sermons on this story. He interprets it as a preoccupation with the finite versus a focus on the infinite, ultimate concern. According to him, Martha's stuck in mundane concerns while Mary directs her attention to what matters most.

For many, certainly for me, the dualism plays out within ourselves. Well into my fourth decade of pastoral ministry, I still struggle, and usually fail, to find the right balance. For example, would Mary have sat in quiet contemplation if mice had been running around under the table and leaving their foul little droppings all over the flowing robes she's usually pictured as wearing? A combination of colder weather and a major construction project across the street disturbed the mice who now found warmth and quiet inside. Mice running around the shelter where residents eat and sleep is not sanitary. They are not welcome guests for Sunday morning coffee hour either. The exterminator declared that everything must be removed from every wall and every closet. He will need a tour of the premises inside and out. Our custodian was not available. The shelter's head social worker was on vacation, and this could not wait until she returned.

The fact that I had just returned from a writing workshop with a clear schedule of time blocked off for extra prayer and writing did not concern the mice, who were masters of distraction. Their only interest appeared to lie with the drawer of onions and potatoes in the kitchen and any food residents had squirreled away in their closets. As for the exterminator, he would arrive at the hour that worked best for him, leaving me to scurry around getting ready for his visit. Of course, all days are not like this, but they arrive more than one would wish. It's easy to feel that contemplation, silence, and writing are luxuries when there are mouths to feed and mice to catch, not to mention (please God, no!) rats.

The writing workshop leader shared numerous nuggets of writerly wisdom, one being that we should write at a steady clip of six hundred words a day. Most days, I'm thrilled with half that. Of course, his plan aims to complete one book per year. My pace has managed to barely produce two books over thirty years, so he has a point. Even more challenging is his conviction that if you want to be a writer, then being a writer must be your primary vocation. Being a pastor may be your job, but being a writer is your identity. Any other job will leave you worried and distracted by many things, when there is need of one thing only, the better part. Yes, being a pastor will bring worries and distractions, some of them scampering around on their tiny, filthy feet, but I can't accept that pastoring is just a job or that writing is just a hobby. They are two inseparable parts of my deepest self, and I can't cut out one without destroying the other.

The same Jesus who said that Mary chose the better part tells us that the chosen of his kin-dom are those who feed the hungry, cloth the naked, welcome strangers, and visit the sick and imprisoned. He teaches the disciples sitting at his feet that just as he washes their dirty feet, they also must stand up and go forth to wash the feet of others. So which is it? What did Jesus mean by saying that Mary has chosen the one thing necessary? Dorothee Sölle, the German liberation theologian, writes, "The history of mysticism is a history of the love for God. I cannot conceive of this without political and praxis-oriented actualization that is directed toward the world." I can't either. Thoughts and prayers are not enough, though we ought to set aside time for prayer.

I try to begin my time of prayer each morning with a psalm, going through the 150 psalms in order. I say "try" because some days I rush out to an appointment with nary a prayer, like Martha on a mission. On my better days, I meditate on the psalm and pick one line that stands out to me from the rest. I could once hold that line in memory to repeat over the course of the day, but that time is long gone. Whatever seemed utterly unforgettable first thing in the morning disappears by noon. Now, I write the line on a small slip of paper and carry it in a pocket or tucked under my clothing close to my heart. I take it out periodically to read, a brief moment of retreat where I can steady myself. In this way, the psalms have become doors that open into sanctuary too. Recently, I've taken to keeping the old slips in a box so that on the busiest of days, I can grab one on the go. This does not uphold the example of Martin Luther, who once said, "I have so much to do that I shall spend the first three hours in prayer," but I tell myself that it's better than nothing.

Every three years, when Martha and Mary step into our sanctuaries through the lectionary—the table of Scripture passages appointed for reading each Sunday—their story is paired with a reading from the prophet Amos that begins: "This is what the Lord God showed me—a basket of summer fruit. He said, 'Amos, what do you see?' And I said, 'A basket of summer fruit'" (Amos 8:1–2). This fruit is not just a sweet addition to the table. It is the introduction to Amos's prophetic rage against those who trample on the needy and bring to ruin the poor of the land.

Did Martha serve fruit to Jesus? To envision the plate of fruit in Martha's hands in light of Amos is to see that what happens in the privacy of our homes and Communion tables is connected to what goes on in the world beyond—where that fruit is grown, how the workers are paid, what pesticides are used. It is to enter into deeper authentic communion with our siblings at the table, sharing sufferings as well as joys and seeing that the prophetic and pastoral are one seamless piece. Most would agree that showing up for a hospital visit is a pastoral act, but showing up at a restaurant picket is a pastoral act for the person who feels alone in the struggle to feed his family. "Never forget," says Cornel West, "that justice is what love looks like in public. We have to recognize that there cannot be relationships unless there is commitment, unless there is loyalty, unless there is love, patience, persistence."

When our stained-glass windows were still displayed in the sanctuary, one depicted the child Jesus holding a blue ruler while shouldering two planks of wood, positioned to form a cross. An art historian told me that the ruler represents the measure of one's character and Lent is often a time when the church urges us to reflect upon how we are measuring up. We measure plenty of things, both helpful and not. We measure a just livable wage and also—did I get to six hundred words? Should I get a prize for twelve hundred and a punishment for taking a whole morning to write one sentence? Am I too active? Too withdrawn? What does it mean that some days I spend more time with the exterminator than praying? Do my days hold too much protest and too little poetry—or the opposite? I find comfort in seeing that Jesus carries his cross along with the blue ruler. I take it as an indication that none of us will ever perfectly measure up, but God's measure is mercy. Maybe, the one thing needful is to remember that.

Comparing ourselves to others is always a temptation. Anybody who knew my mother before the ravages of Parkinson's disease would have described her as a Martha who had no time to sit at anyone's feet. She always kept busy: gardening, cleaning, planning and cooking gourmet meals, creating a home filled with beauty, light, plants, and welcoming comfort. She religiously visited her father, her mother's sister, and my father's sister when, one by one, they were unable to live at home, and she arranged for them to reside in the same nursing home. She chaired church committees and volunteered on community boards. To give a small idea.

She went about each of these activities armed with an intensive program of self-education. For example, in chairing the church's worship committee, most laypeople might brush up on altar guild guides and church seasons. My mother immersed herself in a course of study that exceeded anything I experienced in my seminary worship class. She acquired a set of books that included *The Shape of the Liturgy* by liturgical scholar Dom Gregory Dix. The students in my master's-level seminary class would have balked at being assigned this tome weighing in at 816 pages, but my mother ordered it for herself and then left numerous penciled notes throughout. Her devotion to gardening inspired her to take a class at a nearby university when she felt I was old enough to handle my own homework while she did hers. She'd sit next to me and make intricate drawings of plant cells while I learned about photosynthesis.

She never appeared to tire. Gregorio and I would sink into her comfy couch after a long day and she'd jump up. "I'm playing bee," she'd say, gleefully wielding a tiny paintbush to pollinate her dwarf orange tree, coaxing it into flowering, fruitful glory in the cold New Jersey winter. As I look back, it seems that in being a 1950s stay-at-home housewife and mother, she poured her energies and passions into a vessel far too small, but unlike the biblical Martha, I never heard her complain.

After Ana was born and I had to balance full-time pastoral ministry in the South Bronx with motherhood, while Gregorio also worked full-time, my mother considered our situation and made a decision. She told her pastor that she would no longer be the ever-ready volunteer leader because she wanted to help me at home as her contribution to the church, so that I could follow my pastoral vocation. Once a week, she made the hour trip, driving from New Jersey across the George Washington Bridge into the Bronx to take charge of our home for a day, including overnight. She shopped for us, cleaned for us, fed us, and in time, took both children to school and picked them up. She found random things we needed in a time before Amazon: bags to fit an old vacuum cleaner, an odd replacement dish, hardware to properly hang a picture, the right patch to repair a child's pants. The children had vacation during Holy Week. No problem, Oma was on it. She took the children on outings, getting the materials to dye Easter eggs and the secret makings of Easter baskets. She was always eager to jump on the next project when we just wanted to collapse into a chair. My mother had three decades on us, but often she made us feel old and tired. Once I became a grandmother, my family discussed whether my granddaughter should call me "Oma," as we all recognized that I could never measure up. We decided that I may be called "Oma," although I would be a different one. In any case, at this point, Mia reverses the syllables and calls me "Amo," which means "I love" in Spanish.

Despite my mother's Martha-like activity, she firmly believed in stopping to smell the roses. Literally. On family road trips out west, if we spotted some exotic wildflower growing by the side of the road, she would make sure we pulled over and all got out to enjoy it. Enjoying it also meant toting along guidebooks to identify the flora and fauna in our path. She never failed to remind me that I was too busy and needed my rest. She powered through Parkinson's for many years, but eventually it slowed her down to the point that her legs barely moved and her brain bundled her off on frequent hallucinogenic journeys. Thankfully, she always came back and knew us.

The day began badly. I made the mistake of checking my email before praying and thus started the morning with an angry message from someone who had been excluded from a church email. Then, instead of drinking coffee, I devoted the first few minutes of the seven o'clock hour to cleaning up spilled urine on the second floor. To make the matter more frustrating, I could have prevented the whole ordeal by emptying my mother's commode the previous night instead of letting it wait until the morning when the liquid sloshed over the top. I finally finished with the mess and went to take a shower up on the third floor.

At last I was refreshed, dressed, and ready to start the day again. I was clean, the floor was clean, and the email was sort of cleaned. But my mother was not. She was waiting for me downstairs on the first floor and she asked for a washcloth. It was a perfectly reasonable request, but the washcloth was back up on the third floor. My mother might as well have been telling me to climb Mount Kilimanjaro. I couldn't do it. I was already late and the fact that this additional task was expected of me made me suddenly furious. I knew my anger was misplaced but I was helpless before it.

Soon afterward, in the final weeks of my mother's life, which I didn't realize were the final weeks, she made a peculiar request of Aura, the woman who helped us care for her during the day. My mother had ripped a page from a magazine—I think it was the *New Yorker*—that she was looking through. She could no longer read much but she'd turn the pages. She asked Aura to tape the page to my bedroom door, up the two flights of stairs she could no longer manage. Aura told me this, indicating that she realized it made no sense, but she did it because of my mother's insistence. My mother's page advertised diamond earrings. Aura knew that I don't have pierced ears or crave expensive jewelry.

I wearily climbed the stairs expecting nothing beyond further evidence of my mother's deterioration, nothing beyond an ad for diamond earrings taped to the door. I faced it and instantly saw that it wasn't about the jewelry. Below the diamonds, I read the shining letters, "Become a poet." It was my mother's final gift to me, a brilliant message on the threshold of death: be who you are called to be, do what you are called to do. Do not be distracted by many things.

Holy Week

10

Night of Betrayal

> We're rounding 'em up in a very humane way, in a very nice way. And they're going to be happy because they want to be legalized. And, by the way, I know it doesn't sound nice. But not everything is nice.

It was Holy Thursday and we at Trinity were remembering Jesus's last supper with his disciples. For many years, we've done so with a meal and a celebration of Holy Communion. We've made it tradition to serve a potluck dinner, so we never know exactly how much food or what kind of food will arrive, but usually everything works out. It was working out again, although there wouldn't be many leftovers, and one person who signed up to bring her ever-popular fried chicken didn't show. Then, about halfway through the meal, several dozen homeless men and women came to the door in response to the magic word on the Holy Week flyers we'd hung outside: "Dinner." We scrambled to find room for all to sit and food enough for our new arrivals to eat. We managed. A few people who had just served themselves handed their untouched plates to someone else. Others took half portions, and the woman who came late with the chicken was miraculously right on time.

I awkwardly explained that everyone was welcome but, just so we all knew, this was not actually a community meal like we have on Thanksgiving. It was a worship service. Of course, all were welcome to the worship service, which doubled as a dinner, which confused the people who were just hungry and who had attended community meals in this same space before. And isn't Holy Communion a community meal too?

After eating, we read the story of Jesus washing his disciples' feet and then we wash and dry each other's hands as a sign of honoring service to others. I know quite a few people who disdain handwashing as a poor substitute for the foot washing performed by Jesus, but we have our reasons. One incident in particular pushed me over the edge. A young man tried to persuade his reluctant girlfriend to participate in the foot washing. He insisted that she would find it most meaningful, and she kept repeating that she did not wish to do it. Their disagreement escalated until everyone could hear it, which hardly contributed to the reverent moment. Many people hold back from foot washing, but every person in the room joins in the handwashing without arguing about it.

I find the handwashing moving to watch—children pouring water over the hands of an elder, a homeless man tenderly drying the hands of a teacher, a teenaged boy washing the hands of a mentally challenged woman who beams at him the entire time and in turn, washes the hands of the church treasurer, who washes the hands of a toddler from El Salvador. Of course, no one is actually washing. We don't even use soap as we pour out water and dry each other's hands. But that year, it turned out that people who were really hungry also really wanted to wash. One woman came forward and splashed water on her face while the person before her lifted the towel and gently dried. For her it was not symbolic; she was washing. We say that Holy Communion is not a mere symbol. We say that Jesus is truly present in flesh and blood, even if it looks like bread and wine. And so Jesus was present, even if he looked like a hungry man eating chicken and a hungry woman washing the grime from her face.

A year later, as we gathered for Holy Thursday, Jesus became present in a different way. After the service concluded with the stripping of the altar, I noticed a little girl crying. Since I couldn't reach her immediately, I asked her friends what had happened. Was there a fight? I asked about a fight because there had been one a few weeks earlier in Sunday School. No, no fight. So what was the matter? The little girls kept repeating: "You know, Pastor," but I didn't know. These children had more faith in me than I deserved. When I finally found time to bring the sad child into my office to talk, she said, "It happened to my daddy." This did nothing to enlighten me, dull as I was.

It turned out that a couple of days earlier, some men pounded on her door, stormed the apartment, threw her father to the floor, handcuffed him, and took him away. She had not seen him since and didn't know where he was. I later learned that the men were immigration agents, before the time of ICE, and claimed the arrest had to do with drugs. This little girl instantly connected what she experienced in her apartment with the stripping of the altar, an action that occurred with minimal explanation. Every item around the altar is removed:

standing cross, torches, candles, banners, Bible, altar cloths. The space is stripped bare.

We were following an ancient tradition on Holy Thursday that symbolizes the humiliation of Jesus and the stripping of his garments at the hands of soldiers who finally divested him of his earthly life. Her mother later told me that when her daughter got home after the service, she ran to tell her that what happened to Daddy also happened to Jesus. The worst night of her life was the worst night of his. It was real.

Now stories of parents ripped from the side of their children have become commonplace.

Again, it was a Thursday, though not Holy Thursday, when I answered a call from a friend in the sanctuary movement that trains and coordinates volunteers to accompany and support immigrants in court and in crisis. Some days, the work makes a difference. A member of my church who'd been trained in court accompaniment did what dozens of people do every day at the New York Federal Plaza immigration court: she joined with others in the courtroom when an asylum-seeker went before the judge. The rules required all visitors to sit in silence, which they did, but their presence voiced their testimony. After lawyers for both sides presented their cases, the judge looked up, took in the silent witness, and turned to the man whose fate was being decided for that day: "I see you have family here," she said, and postponed his deportation order.

The call I received that Thursday asked for a person who could be available that very morning and who could speak Spanish. Email requests go out most mornings but it's rare that I can drop everything else to respond. This time I could. A seven-year-old child, Eduardo, had crossed the border from Mexico into El Paso, Texas, with his grandmother hoping to reunite with his mother. ICE apprehended the pair and immediately separated them. They locked the grandmother in a Texas facility and put Eduardo on a plane with strangers to a center in East Harlem where many other child detainees are held. Eduardo arrived at the center in the middle of the night, as is usual, to avoid public attention.

When my friend contacted me, Eduardo had already been separated from his family for three months, and began vomiting up all the food he ate. In recent weeks, Eduardo had ceased eating altogether, became seriously ill, and was hospitalized. His mother was outside the radar of ICE, but the grandmother got permission to visit for two weeks in order to convince the little boy to eat. ICE allowed it only because of outreach from the sanctuary movement who had been trying to track the child down, and because they didn't want to have a child's death on their hands. People in the movement arranged for Eduardo's grandmother and mother to travel to New York.

I was told that I would meet with the grandmother at a chosen location, but when I arrived, Eduardo's mother was there too. The desperate women poured out their story, which contradicted much of the public rhetoric on family separations. When his mother tried to speak with Eduardo on the phone and get the address of where he was being held, the social worker refused to help her. Eventually, Eduardo was released from the hospital and allowed to visit with his family for two hours a day, but not on weekends because there were not enough staff to supervise. Eduardo was not allowed off the premises of the center, treated like a prisoner, rather than a traumatized seven-year-old who cries every day when his family leaves and then again refuses to eat.

The room where Eduardo slept was basically a closet with a bunk bed. His mother and grandmother could barely squeeze into the space. They told me that Eduardo had bruises on his head where older boys hit him, although the staff insisted that they tried to keep the older and younger children apart. Presently, the center is one of many under investigation for the sexual abuse of the children in its care.

According to the Department of Justice, children were to be reunited with their families as soon as the family could be located, but even though Eduardo's family had arrived, he was not allowed to return to them. The government required fingerprints and DNA testing to prove that the mother was not a criminal or stranger trying to traffic him, even though she had his birth certificate from Mexico and he wailed for her, "MAMA! MAMA!" She was told it could take a month to get the fingerprint report back, but one month passed and then two and now nobody knows. The DNA test was allegedly missing.

Eduardo stayed in a much better physical environment than the children held in filthy cages. He had an actual bed and meals. But the food he ate was no better than crackers, which is all that the children closer to the border receive, because his extreme distress didn't allow him to keep anything down. There is nothing "better" achieved by seizing a child from a loving family. The only bright spots in this long night of betrayal were the people of faith rallying to help, locating family members, buying tickets for them to travel, and providing hospitality for the mother and grandmother in New York.

After I met with the grandmother and mother, listened to their story, offered the prayers they requested, and took them to find Mexican food for Eduardo, they asked me to take them to the center where Eduardo was being held captive. Before we could go, a member of a synagogue, also active in the Sanctuary network, pulled up in his car, having volunteered and been scheduled to drive them to see Eduardo on that day and drive them back. I don't know where Eduardo is now. Many of the children at the East Harlem center are sent to foster care with no promise that they will ever return to their families. There are stars that shine as this night of betrayal drags on, but no sign of dawn.

11

Credible Fear

> It's a big fat con job, folks.

I smelled. After spending seven hours in close proximity with families who have not been able to wash in weeks, my own hair and clothing had absorbed the odor. On the train ride back to where I was staying in San Diego, I noticed that people avoided the seat next to me, until the unfortunate woman who saw no other choice. What could I say? I'm sorry, but this is the aroma of hope and desperation? This is the scent of national cruelty? I said nothing, put in earphones, and closed my eyes.

When the New Sanctuary Movement put out a call for clergy to visit the border during a time of increasing hysteria over invading caravans, my congregation encouraged me to go. They wanted me to see the truth firsthand and come back to share it with them. I spent two weeks in San Diego and Tijuana near the San Isidro port of entry, the busiest border crossing between the United States and Mexico.

During my first week, an ecumenical organization in San Diego tasked me with documenting information for families who had been found crossing somewhere other than the official port of entry. These families were apprehended and taken to detention centers for several days where they were given only orange peanut butter crackers to eat before being strapped with electronic ankle monitors, loaded into buses by ICE, and dropped off at random locations with nothing but paperwork indicating when and where they should appear in court. Giselle and her eight-year-old daughter were among those picked up by volunteers who drove around looking for stranded families. It was an unnecessary cruelty that it was always after dark, often late, that the families were left somewhere. After passing through a medical triage tent run by volunteer nurses, Giselle and her daughter came to the room where I sat with a computer.

While her daughter colored pictures of birds, Giselle told me about the video dropped off by a local gang when she lived back home in El Salvador. The recording showed her brother being tortured, murdered, and dismembered with a machete. A note promised the same for her and her child if they did not disappear. As she choked up while telling me this story, a volunteer came by with bottled water. Giselle then told me about her sister who sold bags of water in San Salvador to help support her three children. This sister had been kidnapped, stripped, and raped by a gang who left her wounded and naked miles outside of her village. Giselle worried about her sister who stayed back home, fearing the trip would be too difficult with three children, including an infant.

When Giselle finished sharing what she wanted documented, it was time to call the person she was going to stay with while awaiting court proceedings. Everyone who was released had the number and address of a person they could stay with somewhere in the United States. Part of my job was to call these persons in what might be the middle of the night in their time zone and explain how to transfer a plane or bus ticket to the family member or friend in San Diego. It became much more complicated if the person on the other end of the phone did not have access to a computer or a credit card. In those cases, a staff member would step in to help determine other options.

The system can break down easily. If a sponsor changes her mind or cannot be reached, another friend or family member might be found, but instead of in Boston, the newly identified relative might be in Birmingham. Technically, this is permitted, but the court date was already set for Boston and changing it is nearly impossible. Furthermore, the ankle monitors are preset with GPS tracking that sends an alarm if they turn up somewhere other than stated in the original paperwork. Even if a person ends up in his original location, the immigration court assigned might be hours away from where a person is staying, with no public transportation to get there. The pastor who hosted me once drove someone four hours to an appointment, but most people do not know anyone so generous with their time and who can take off time from work to drive.

After seeing dozens of families, I couldn't remember what arrangements were made for Giselle. What I do remember is the story she wanted heard, and I remember how she wanted to be remembered. After she and I finished documenting her story, Giselle and her daughter left to eat, bathe, and change into fresh clothes. Giselle had already apologized for being dirty. She'd had no chance to bathe since leaving home in El Salvador and was not permitted to wash at the detention facility. Following their showers, everyone was supposed to head directly to another area with beds, to make room for new families in the room where I logged information. Nonetheless, Giselle broke protocol and insisted on returning to me because she did not want to be remembered as a victim caked with grime. And so I remember Giselle and her daughter, damp and smiling, the little girl now fed and fragrant with shampoo, clutching her drawing of birds.

Eventually, Giselle will face "a credible fear interview." All asylum-seekers must try to convince people who are not likely to believe them that their life is in danger and it is not safe for them to return to their country of origin. Although the president repeatedly labels immigrants as criminals and con artists, my experience with dozens of parents and children arriving at our border is that they are far more likely to be the victims of violent crimes. Lacking police reports or other supporting evidence, I met many asylum-seekers hoping to offer their scarred bodies as testimony. "Unless I see the mark of the nails in his hands, and put my finger in the mark of the nails and my hand in his side, I will not believe" (John 20:24) said the disciple Thomas, in words referring to Jesus's body ravaged by crucifixion, words that have taken on a new meaning for me.

When Giselle and her daughter left to find their beds, I met Julissa and her three-year-old son from Honduras. When Julissa was seven, her mother died and she went to live with an aunt and cousin who put her to work doing all the cleaning, cooking, and washing while being verbally and physically abused. A year ago, her cousin sliced the right side of her face from ear to jawbone because she had left something unwashed. She lifted her shirt and showed me the scar on her side where he'd cut her a second time. She had lost a lot of blood and tried to file a report, but the police waved her away. Having nowhere to go, Julissa stayed on, but recently, the cousin began to regularly beat her little boy. When she protested, he threatened to kill them both if they didn't get out of the house. They fled Honduras and now sat before me.

Julissa wanted me to consider the dark red scars on her face. She lifted her T-shirt and asked me to examine her side. Are the scars bad enough? Are they healing too well? We have turned the border into a place where scars of abuse and violence are treasured to prove credible fear. I also encountered a number of people with broken legs, the result of climbing a border fence and falling to the other side. One man shattered his leg on a rock, and his ability to get the proper care on either side of the border was in doubt. "Should you not know justice?" the prophet Micah wrote, "you who hate the good and love the evil, who tear the skin off my people, and . . . break their bones in pieces" (Mic 3:1–3).

After spending my nights at this refuge in San Diego, I was asked to go to Tijuana. Immigrants arrive there legally to ask for asylum but are kept waiting for months before they are allowed to present themselves. Once they do, they face untold time in detention and often family separation. I was asked to wear recognizable clerical garb and to simply be available for prayer for those who requested it. People came to this location to get legal information and support, food, and to rest as they waited to start the asylum process. A playroom with toys and art supplies offered a distraction for children who became bored with hour upon hour of waiting.

The first person who approached me was a transgender Mexican woman who had been beaten nearly to death. It occurred to me that she might not be much safer in the United States, but I did not mention that. After praying freely, I read a prayer that has always been meaningful to me. In English it says:

> O God, you have called your servants to ventures
> of which we cannot see the ending,
> by paths as yet untrodden, through perils unknown.
> Give us faith to go out with good courage, not knowing where we go,
> but only that your hand is leading us and your love supporting us,
> through Jesus Christ our Lord. Amen.

She asked me if she could have a copy to keep with her. I wrote it out for her, and she pressed a flower made from a braided palm frond into my hand. Many others asked me to write down the words to prayers and psalms I shared with them. It reminded me of base communities in Argentina where the laypeople who planned worship would write out the words to songs by hand multiple times for the congregation to use.

Most of those I prayed with were families from Central America. Many migrants from Cameroon also arrived in Tijuana after a lengthy, dangerous journey on two continents, expecting to simply present themselves for asylum at the port. The wait stretched on indefinitely, and the Africans ran out of money with no place to stay and no way to return. I learned that Cameroon's English-speaking minority is denied employment and faces increasing violence without legal recourse. They, too, will have to prove that their fear is credible and they will have to find a way to survive in Tijuana in the meantime.

While praying, we could hear a man shouting. A young volunteer tried to calm him down but finally brought him to me. I wondered what he thought I could do. I had trouble understanding the man who was wailing, moaning, and saying something about being beaten by the police. I couldn't tell if he was drunk or had been pushed over a mental edge. He was a Mexican national with no interest in immigration, but had wandered in, perhaps seeking some respite from the street. Instead, he became increasingly agitated, adding to the already high level of stress for everyone else and frightening the children.

I remembered why I was there and interrupted his tirade to ask if he would like to pray. I didn't count on the impact of those words as this deranged man schooled me in the power of prayer. He instantly quieted, nodded, and folded his hands. After we prayed, he received the Communion host I held out, swallowed, and immediately fell asleep. I thought of my granddaughter who falls asleep after nursing:

> I do not occupy myself with things
> too great and too marvelous for me.
> But I have calmed and quieted my soul,
> like a weaned child with its mother;
> my soul is like the weaned child that is with me.
>
> Psalm 131: 1b–2

For others, sleep is deadly. Julio traveled with his wife and three children from Guatemala because the government seized his land, leaving him with no means to grow food to feed his family. Julio wanted to speak and pray in private, so we brought two metal folding chairs to a corner of the crowded room. He told me that he and his family had ridden *La Bestia,* or "The Beast," a name given to the freight trains that run from southern Mexico to the northern border. Migrants from Central America climb atop the trains and hold on for dear life. Some call them "trains of death" due to the danger of falling off and being dismembered on the tracks. The peril has grown over time as Mexico tries to deter this practice by increasing the speed of the trains.

Julio told me that he saw five people killed when they fell asleep and rolled off. He twisted T-shirts into blindfolds for his children to wear so that they wouldn't see. He and his wife took turns staying awake and holding on to the children. The family looked exhausted and gaunt from hunger, but their desperation yielded no visible scars that might prove credible fear and win asylum. Fearing the beast of poverty does not count under a regime where tax cuts to help the poor by creating "opportunity zones" in economically depressed communities actually function as a windfall for the rich, and not just any rich. According to the *New York Times*, "The tax break is largely benefiting the real estate industry—where Mr. Trump made his fortune and still has extensive business interests—and it is luring people with personal or professional connections to the president." In such a landscape, the beast of poverty cannot provoke credible fear because it's no more than a chimera. Its victims vanish in desert sands and behind bars, in hidden and distant places anywhere but here.

Easter

12

Pupusas at the Tomb

> We` re going to build a wall, folks. We` re going to build a wall. That wall will go up so fast, your head will spin.

Before leaving Tijuana, I spent a day volunteering with the World Central Kitchen, a wonderful "Chefs without Borders" organization where I met Trini. Back in El Salvador, Trini had worked in a restaurant preparing her specialty *pupusas*—thick, cornmeal flatbread stuffed with cheese, meat, or refried beans. Trini's boss went away for a time and left her in charge of the restaurant. Before long, a gang member broke in and held a gun to her head, demanding that she pay them $500 a month, a common form of extortion. Trini explained to the unbelieving gang leaders that she did not own the restaurant and couldn't pay. Before leaving, they shot Trini in the upper arm and warned that next time they would shoot her in the head. Trini fled within days. She didn't dare travel to say good-bye to her twenty-year-old son, fearing that she was being watched and her visit might endanger his life.

Trini now waited in Tijuana to present herself for asylum. While staying in a shelter, she received meals through the World Central Kitchen and soon offered to volunteer. Her culinary gifts were quickly recognized, earning her a safe place to stay and a stipend. I first met her after she noticed me in the kitchen, struggling to keep up with the pace of prepping over a thousand meals. Trini was on what she considered a break and she invited me to sit beside her as she demonstrated her method of folding napkins around spoons. Her dark hair was held up in a shower cap, as was mine. She paused to show me the wound where the gang's bullet entered her arm, hoping, like so many others, that the scar will prove her case.

After a day chopping onions, folding napkins, and watching her work with a smile that rarely left her face, it was clear that Trini was not doing this only for the money. I saw a woman engaged in defiant resistance, refusing to be objectified by pity or dehumanized as a criminal. Like Jesus, in the face of betrayal, Trini holds out bread. In the face of suffering, Trini rises at dawn to bake bread to feed the hungry multitudes. With her wounded arms, she offers life. She nourishes hope.

During my time at the border, I saw no children in cages, but I saw the geography of Good Friday with shackles and barbed wire, sharp and cruel as a crown of thorns, stretched before me on every side. Guards and guns, sweat and fear closed in, but none of it could stop the stubborn belief that Easter was coming. In fact, Easter was already there, pulsing in a throng of waiting hearts. As Clarence Jordan once said: "The good news of the resurrection of Jesus is not that we shall die and go home to be with him, but that he has risen and comes home to us, bringing all his hungry, naked, thirsty, sick prisoner brothers with him."

When I came back home and shared photos and stories from the border, Trinity worship planners were inspired to bring the reality closer to the full congregation's awareness in a visceral way. They put out a call for volunteers to help with a painting project. We ordered two seven-foot-high canvas room dividers and gathered a group of artistically inclined people and others who simply brought their willingness to pick up a paintbrush. The task was to replicate a section of the border wall based on a photo I took. Painting the metal slats of the wall occupied those with no special painterly skill, and one of our artists led a few others to fill in details of the desert background. After two intensive Saturday sessions with breaks for pizza, we had our wall.

We placed the wall at the entrance of the sanctuary, on either side of our central aisle. No one could enter the church without facing it. Our baptismal font stood in the entrance as well, in the middle of the dividing wall. We filled it with sand to represent the desert and placed a bowl of water on top. We wrapped the font in barbed wire, a scandalous reminder that our holiest things have, at times, been hideously perverted.

As people entered the space and passed through the wall on their way to find a seat, they could read some explanatory material:

> The walls ahead represent the walls on our southern border, a reminder of the many walls that divide us from God and from one another. . . . The sand in our baptismal font represents the desert where God's children continue to perish for lack of water and lack of compassion. You are invited to touch the water as a reminder of the life-giving promises God pours out in baptism.

I understand that walls, barbed wire, and nativity sets in dog cages are not the preferred direction of liturgical arts in most congregations. I visited one of our church members who now resides in a nursing home. Peter's eyes lit up when he saw me, and he excitedly began to tell me about his latest adventure. Apparently, Trump had moved into the fifth floor of the nursing home and Peter was livid. It was intolerable that Trump should invade his space like this. After many months of acclimating, Peter had finally settled into the home and found a measure of peace there, but now Trump turned up and spoiled everything. Peter told me he complained repeatedly to supervisors and administrators and that, thanks to his persistence, the staff agreed to move Trump to a different floor. As Peter shared about his relief and his hero-status among the other fifth-floor residents, we sat in a common room with an enormous TV. I will allow you to guess what larger-than-life face was beaming down on us throughout our conversation. Peter may have had increasing signs of dementia, but he was not wrong. Don't we all feel that Trump has moved into our headspace, if not our homes?

Many of us are like Peter. We want to enter our sanctuaries, settle down, and find some of the peace that passes understanding. Church worship can offer longed-for respite from our problems, both personal and national. We need such time to step away as Jesus did, even if he was often interrupted by anxious disciples and needy crowds before he was ready for them. All of this suggests the paradoxical nature of sanctuary.

The rabbis, who knew something about Sabbath rest, instruct in the Talmud: "Never pray in a room without windows." To me, this means that prayer is relational, nurturing my relationship with God and simultaneously drawing me closer to the world around me. Prayer is not an escape, but rather a deepening of connections. Can we say we offer sanctuary, if our actual fears, struggles, doubts, hurts, and anger must be left outside the doors? If we deliberately close our minds and hearts from considering the suffering of those beyond our windows and walls? Will a queer person feel safe and seen if we fly a rainbow flag outside but neglect to light candles and pray for the victims of Pulse inside? Can Black Lives Matter if attacks on the Black community are not repudiated, visibly grieved, or even mentioned in church?

It's remarkable that people who gather to worship in spaces with a cross prominently displayed become upset about politics in the sanctuary. No matter what meaning we find in the cross, what theory of atonement we adhere to, the cross represents a tool of political oppression and suppression. The Roman Empire used the cross as an instrument of torture and punishment. As one of my childhood pastors used to say, "Jesus was not crucified on a golden cross between two candlesticks." Yet many worshippers do not view the cross as disturbing the peace. We are used to it. We are not used to walls and barbed wire in our sanctuaries. We are not used to seeing the faces of trans women or the names of murdered Black men and boys on our crosses. These things should shock us not for shock's sake, but to force us to face the horror that attends the act of crucifixion on Golgotha and the continued suffering of God's children.

This does not mean that worship merely rehashes the news. I enter a church sanctuary hoping to find some Holy Spirit perspective. I arrive in need of fresh hope and inspiration born of lament, repentance, prayer, and praise, but not a spell of amnesia. We need times for contemplative prayer that differ from our communal Sunday morning worship, but even contemplative prayer is not a practice for mystical escape artists. The word "contemplate" comes from the Latin *contem-*

platus, "to gaze attentively," "to observe," from *com*, "together" plus *templum*, "temple." Contemplation requires a time and space set aside for the act of looking deeply into the nature of things.

The talmudic scholar Rabbi Yohanan connects the advice to pray with open windows to a line in the book of Daniel: "he continued to go to his house, which had windows in its upper room open toward Jerusalem, and to get down on his knees three times a day to pray to his God" (Daniel 6:10). It's interesting that Daniel's prayer in this room is an act of civil disobedience that will cause the king to throw him to the lions. Daniel was a Jew exiled in Babylon, where the king had just signed a law forbidding anyone to pray to any god or human other than the king himself. Although Daniel knew that the document had been signed, he continued to go to his house with open windows in its upper room, and to get down on his knees three times a day to pray to his God—in defiance of the law of the land.

I believe that the detail of windows open toward Jerusalem illuminates a deeper meaning to the Talmudic instruction. Besides openness to the cries of the world around us, to look to Jerusalem means to fix our sight on the future, to look toward the dawning of a new day. For Christians, it means to keep before us a vision of Easter, of new creation, of the world as God intends it, without tyrannical kings or messianic presidents.

Our wall stood throughout the season of Lent and Holy Week, but our worship team decided to remove it on Easter, when our focus as a community shifts from crucifixion to resurrection. Rather than disassemble it in private, though, they thought to include it in the resurrection-day service. As the chords of our opening hymn rang through the colorful, bombinating crowds of Easter with every child clutching a little bell, we heard the words:

> But now in Christ Jesus you who once were far off have been brought near by the blood of Christ. For he is our peace; in his flesh he has made both groups into one and has broken down the dividing wall, that is, the hostility between us. . . . So then you are no longer strangers and aliens, but you are citizens with the saints and also members of the household of God. (Ephesians 2:13–14, 19)

And then, as everyone turned to face the festive procession of worship leaders and we sang out the first of many alleluias, each accompanied by eager bell-ringers, a team dismantled the panels of the wall and danced them away like the angels who once removed a massive stone in a garden where the stakes of life and death were everything.

13

Dance Party

Under the Trump administration, the State Department, the Department of Justice, the Department of Health and Human Services, the Department of Housing and Urban Development, the Department of Defense, the Bureau of Prisons and the Department of Education have all sought to rescind protections for transgender persons.

In the weeks before Trinity's stained-glass windows were scheduled for removal, I preached a sermon series based on their images and got stuck on one, unable to identify the story it told. The window in question depicted a young person who appeared in their late teens or early twenties, shrouded in burial sheets. The cloth falls away from the glass face just enough to reveal dark hair and ghostly bruises around the eyes. An older woman, whom I assumed to be the mother, has matching dark circles under her eyes. She is beside the young person who reclines on a bed that has been carried and set before Jesus on the stones of a public square. The woman stretches out both arms, imploring this healer to save her child's life.

Jesus stands between them and grasps the limp fingers of the youth while placing a steadying hand on the mother's shoulder. The youth is not quite awake, but no longer dead. The people with them express various types of astonishment. One scratches his head. One stares. One prays. A young man points to the bed while looking into the face of the elder beside him to make sure he has seen this marvel. A woman with bulging eyes holds her head in her hands as if it might fall off.

I couldn't settle on what biblical story I was seeing in the window because I couldn't tell if the youth was male or female. This disturbed me as I walked around the sanctuary, scrutinizing the window from various angles, at different times of day, looking for markers of gender I couldn't find. In the thin light of an early winter's morning, I saw him as a young man, but by afternoon when the sun shone brightly, she would appear as a young woman. Gender shifted with the weather. How could I preach without the right pronouns? Finally, it dawned on me that I was more focused on pronouns than healing. This happened years before nonbinary pronouns like *ze* and *hir* entered the dictionary—or my vocabulary. At that time I also struggled to use "they" in the singular for those who preferred it.

A dozen years ago, when we opened Trinity Place, the "T" in LGBTQ was just a letter. We had church members who identified as gay, lesbian, or bisexual, but not transgender, at least, not to my knowledge. I'd never given much thought to those who understand themselves as genderqueer or nonbinary, although I did remember my piano teacher at Brown in 1972 who met me at the door of the music department in heels and a flowing, flowered skirt paired with a man's pinstripe oxford shirt and beard. This startled me on the first day of class, and then we moved on to Mozart.

It came as a surprise when over a third of our shelter residents identified as transgender, but it shouldn't have. In their churches, the healer in our window has been converted into a soul-shredding demonizer smartly suited up for his pulpit from which parents get their marching orders to rid their homes of filth. No wonder many of the youth who come through our doors have attempted or considered suicide.

Over the years, the shelter residents taught me through their stories. I witnessed their pain when mis-gendered intentionally and received their grace when I did it by accident. I came to see and understand that while some would do anything possible to pass as the gender they identified with, others defiantly refused gender norms. As far as pronouns go, the best thing to do is ask. Zoe's pronouns are she, her, and hers, the same as mine, except that Zoe's are far more costly.

I went to the hospital following her gender-confirmation surgery knowing she would have no mother at her bedside. The sister who promised to come was busy vacationing on the beach in Florida. When I arrived, Zoe was being wheeled off for a second surgery due to complications. Later, she told me it was more painful than anything in her life, worse than a childhood of being locked in closets, burned with cigarettes, and sexually molested. Now she sat up in bed, untangling her long, auburn hair, spread out against the white pillows, and described feeling utterly liberated. She looked in the mirror and saw at last what she'd longed for since she was three years old: a body that matches who she truly is.

I left the room to get some fresh ice water for Zoe and came back to find her friend Sofie sitting on the hospital bed. She was on her way to work, wearing a black polka-dot dress cinched with a pink patent-leather belt. Lacy fringe rimmed the edge of the skirt over black tights.

Sofie's dark hair was pulled back from her face with a turban headband, topped with a big, red bow. The skirt was short, but not too short, as she wanted to look professional for her new job. Sofie was employee of the month at Starbucks until she was fired after coworkers complained that her presence made them uncomfortable. At the time, this was legal discrimination and it remains lawful in most states, but not presently in New York. After many miserable months of getting up and getting ready to face interviewers who would barely meet her eyes, Sofie began work as a beauty consultant, where her talents were appreciated and nobody cared where she used the bathroom. She and Zoe launched into an intense debate on the virtues of various eye shadows, and I left so they could have some private time together.

During their stay at the shelter, Sofie and Zoe both asked to be baptized. Unlike Zoe, Sofie had already been baptized with what is called her dead name, a name that held no life or truth for her, and so she longed to be rebaptized with her real name and gender. Dead-naming plagues many of the transgender young people who arrive here. Under the Trump administration, the push to remove protections for transgender persons extends to the attempted erasure of their very existence. In December of 2017, the Centers for Disease Control and Prevention instructed its staff not to use certain words in official documents. These words included "transgender," "vulnerable," and "diversity."

I suggested to Sofie that another baptism wasn't necessary since God always knew her deepest self, but we could do an affirmation of baptism with her true name. And so it was that Zoe and Sofie stood beside the font. Tears and baptismal water ran together, and then I anointed their radiant faces with oil and added the words: "Rejoice that your name is written in heaven." They stood together, holding their candles and basking in the congregation's applause. Afterward we had cake, and they posed for photos like models in their slinky black dresses, beaming and breathtaking.

Zoe and Sofie reminded us all that the waters of baptism, like the waves of the Red Sea, part for the sake of our liberation from everything that would drown out our true selves, from every category that imprisons us. Trans young people are not the only ones who live with the pain of a closeted identity, of not fitting into familial or societal expectations, but brave, trans young people have much to teach the church about resistance, resilience, and resurrection.

It's hard for me to think of Sofie and Zoe as privileged but they know differently. While Zoe lay in her hospital bed the day after her second surgery, and nothing seemed easy, she said, "I know it's easier for me because I'm white. Others have it worse." She was right. We have a marble angel in the back of the sanctuary who wears a paper shawl draped over winged shoulders. The shawl is covered with photos of women's faces and serves as a memorial for transgender women murdered in the United States. Almost all of them are women of color, mostly Black. The average life span for these women is thirty-five.

Nikki is one who narrowly escaped with her life. She required reconstructive facial surgery after being pummeled on a Brooklyn sidewalk by a group of young men who also left her with permanent brain damage. Although our shelter usually closes during the day when residents are out working, studying, or have options at various day programs, we made an exception for Nikki, who recovered in a quiet room off our sanctuary under the watchful eyes of Elmo the turtle, whose own gender was reassigned after Elmo laid an egg. Both Nikki and Elmo were surrounded by a bevy of angels drawn by our preschoolers, including my favorite angel with the body of a mermaid and wings in the place of fins lifting her to the clouds.

We know that being pummeled by psychological trauma leaves an imprint too. When I first met Zoe, she appeared timid and reserved, barely speaking, but inside the righteous furies of trauma raged. Following surgery, she spoke of a slow transmutation of anger become a pillar of fire to lead the way forward. When Zoe recovers from her surgery and removes all the bandages, she has plans to rise up, like the youth in our window did, and begin a job organizing for trans rights and helping others like herself find housing. She will do this part-time for the foreseeable future because the work of healing burns up considerable energy too.

Recently, while visiting Germany, I came across a series of sixteenth-century paintings at churches in Wittenberg and Leipzig. One of the more famous paintings in St. Mary's Church of Wittenberg depicts the scene from our window: *The Resurrection of the Widow's Son from Nain*, painted by Lucas Cranach in 1569. A large procession of townspeople accompany the widow and a cluster of women stand beside her, all dressed in black and all with white bandages pulled over their mouths. Similarly bandaged women appear in other paintings in regional churches I visited and in Wittenberg's town hall.

These depictions of women with their mouths tightly banded shut simultaneously horrified and riveted me. I first thought, standing beside the Cranach, that these women were nuns who had taken a vow of silence, although some of the paintings showed the women standing among family members, including children. I eventually learned that all the women with bandages over their mouths were widows, bound to silence because they didn't have a man to oversee their speech. Should any legal testimony be required of them, a male relative would be their mouthpiece. Their shut-up mouths were also a sign of their closeted sexuality. A widowed woman had to keep silent for at least a year before being allowed to remarry—all lips closed tight. The German word for it is *mundtot*, or "mouth dead." The women who suffered the loss of their spouses could not wail in grief. Not even a sigh of sadness could escape their bound lips. Certainly, they could utter no opinion, complaint, or protest over the violence of war that turned so many of them into widowed dead mouths.

The widow in Cranach's painting is dressed as a well-off, sixteenth-century German, but her forced silence binds her to countless women through the ages, women widowed by violence, mothers bereft at the hands of racist hate crimes, their suffering and testimony ignored in an unending succession of trials and verdicts. Some, including sexual-assault survivors, receive settlements that stifle speech as surely as medieval bandages. Their tongues are like a cancer on the body politic, or the body of Christ, to be surgically removed. When her son is raised up, the widow cannot even laugh aloud for joy and the word "transgender" is erased from officially sanctioned vocabulary.

Our stained-glass window of healing now sits in a basement closet, but stories of healing abound. The story in our undercroft shelter is filled with loud noise and laughter, boisterous meetings, and frequent protests. On any night, an impromptu dance party might break out. Zoe turns up the music. Sofie yells across the room and uproarious laughter ensues. Others make chicken wings in the kitchen. They hold spatulas up to their mouths like microphones and sing. This is the sound of revolution. The beds have been wheeled out, but remain empty, since all the young people are up—eating, talking, dancing, and laughing at once. The bandages have been ripped off.

Pentecost

14

Better Than Dolls

Why are we having all these people from shit hole countries come here, we should have more people from countries like Norway?

As a child, I adored Pentecost. Of course, I looked forward to the delights of Christmas and Easter, but Pentecost was close behind as a favorite church holiday even though it came with no presents to unwrap and no sparkly decorations. It brought no colored eggs or baskets filled with sweets. Pentecost treats of any kind did not exist. My love sprung purely from the power of story—and likely the excitement of my parents. Pentecost is a big day in Germany, where my father grew up. The following Monday is a national holiday and the peonies that bloom in late spring when Pentecost falls are called *Pfingstrosen*, or Pentecost roses. As the head of our church's worship committee, my mother always insisted on special Pentecost flower arrangements and banners, which I sometimes helped her create. I remember her putting leaf extensions into our dining room table in order to roll out a large swath of magenta felt that formed the background for big pink-and-white-ribboned packages representing gifts of the Spirit.

The Pentecost story in the book of Acts recounts the coming of the Holy Spirit to Jesus's disciples after Jesus was no longer bodily present. A rush of wind and tongues of fire rocked the room in which they gathered and they "began to speak in other languages, as the Spirit gave them ability. . . . And at this sound the crowd gathered and was bewildered, because each one heard them speaking in the native language of each" (Acts 2:4, 6). Pentecost is celebrated as the church's birthday, the beginning of a new community—a new Spirit-filled people that embraces not only all nations, but all ages and classes:

> I will pour out my Spirit upon all flesh,
> and your sons and your daughters shall prophesy,
> and your young men shall see visions,
> and your old men shall dream dreams.
> Even upon my slaves, both men and women,
> in those days I will pour out my Spirit;
> and they shall prophesy. (Acts 2:17–18)

Something about the global nature of Pentecost inspired me. I had a great-aunt who traveled the world and sent me a doll from every country she visited. She actually sent two, one for me and one for my only girl cousin. Most of these dolls, in their intricate costumes, were meant to be gazed upon rather than played with, especially the one from Thailand, swathed in glittery, golden fabric. She wore a tall, pointed, very fragile headdress covered in jewels and her slippers looked like woven diamonds. She stood forever poised as if in the middle of a dance. All the dolls arrived at my address and I got to pick the one I wanted before sending the other to my cousin. She was two years older; I looked up to her and tried to send her the doll I thought she'd prefer. But when the two dolls from Thailand arrived, one in gold and one in green, I guiltily kept the golden one for myself.

The dolls sat safely on their shelves in my bedroom throughout the year until the day of Pentecost. Then I took them from their places and set them up in a large circle on our living room carpet for their yearly Pentecost dance party. An only child, I invited my parents to witness the fun. I remember them toasting the dancing dolls with a glass of wine and allowing me to have a tall glass of ginger ale, something reserved for special occasions.

The dolls who managed to survive my childhood, including the golden girl in her headdress, wait behind glass to see what my granddaughter, Mia, will choose to do with them when she's older. I don't recall my own children getting excited about the dolls, although they enjoyed Pentecost for different reasons. They liked getting up early on Pentecost morning to go to church and use a helium tank to blow up red balloons that we tied to the ends of every pew. They had more fun swallowing some of the gas in order to talk back and forth in squeaky hilarity than they did playing with the dolls.

Now I tried to communicate Pentecost joy to new generations. At Trinity, the red balloons arrived already filled. As Pentecost worship began, children entered with long, red ribbons swirling through the air on tall bendable poles, and they somehow managed to keep the ribbons from tangling with the balloons. Children acted out the drama with whooshing sounds for the wind and red, orange, and yellow streamers that flamed over their heads. The celebration was multilingual as befitted the biblical story of people coming from around the world and hearing the disciples speak in their own language. In the native tongues of those present, we heard, "Come, Holy Spirit" in Amharic and Swahili, Turkish, French, Chinese,

Arabic, German, Spanish, Italian, Portuguese, and Dutch. It was better, even, than dolls.

For Communion, we shared fragrant Eritrean bread brought forward by Gennet, who wore a flowing white and gold gown from her native land. A little girl who had made it through the desert and across the border wore new light-up sneakers that blinked as she walked around lighting the altar candles. She eyed the red balloons hovering above the pews but knew she must wait until later to take one home. Afterward, we had birthday cake and sang "Happy Birthday" to the church. As we celebrated the breath of God moving in our midst, others sat in the ER with asthma. Trump's eager dismantling of climate-change protections will only serve to make it harder to breathe.

One Old Testament reading for Pentecost Sunday is the story of the Tower of Babel built when "the whole earth had one language and the same words" (Gen. 11:1). It sounds like an English-only paradise with no room for misunderstandings or confusion, no differences of perspective, and no diversity. When I first learned the story, I was taught that God scattered the people around the world with different languages as a punishment for the arrogance of trying to build a tower up to heaven. But with gorgeous, mind-blowing diversity built into every aspect of God's creation, why would God use difference of language and location as a punishment? In Genesis 1, God commands people to be fruitful and multiply and fill the earth. If God wanted people to fill the earth, wouldn't sending them throughout the earth a few chapters later serve as a positive thing, a fulfillment of purpose? Maybe the problem here is that people were building a closed tower in a gated city where diversity of language and opinion is not allowed and difference in experience is not acknowledged? Isn't that a description of totalitarianism? Maybe God scatters the people of Babel to fill the earth with diverse languages and cultures as originally intended.

The miracle of Pentecost is not that everyone speaks one language but that as people gather from all over the world, speaking many different languages, they understand one another. In the midst of varied identities and experiences, each has their place in the dance. Except in Trump's America, which glorifies English only. If he could, Trump would put a stop to Pentecost. He marked Pentecost Monday of 2017 by celebrating his travel ban and denouncing the Department of Justice for "watering it down." At Trinity, a stilt dancer swooped in with wide wings rising almost as high as our tall columns, a towering height that Trump will never achieve.

Trinity Sunday

15

Team Effort

> Here's the thing. I don't have teams, everyone's talking about teams . . . I'm the team.

People come to Trinity because praying and singing with others still uplifts the spirit and stirs the soul. They come to share in the company of others doing what can't be done as well alone—like sheltering those without homes—or finding such shelter. They come to hear what one congregant likes to call "impolite preaching," which another says "points straight through the bullshit of doctrine where rules overrun right and justice and grace." And they come because of the words of Jesus: "where two or three are gathered in my name, I am there among them" (Matt. 18:20). That promise, I see over and over at Trinity, takes flesh as we commune with bread and wine and with one another.

Following the 2016 election, many churches I know experienced what they called "a Trump bump," an increase in numbers. It seemed that the need to belong to a community of shared values mattered more than ever. But maybe, following the election, we also needed spaces where we could gather with people we differed from. At Trinity, we share many beliefs and values, but there remains much that we do not share. No matter who you are, when you arrive at Trinity, you encounter a range of difference surrounding you in the pews. If you are put off by such difference, you're not likely to stay. A grad student doing research on sex, gender, and worms at a Columbia University lab, a mother of four boys trying to keep her sons away from neighborhood gangs who've already beat up her boyfriend, and an immigrant from Eritrea sit and sing near each other, yet embody the divisions of our larger society. We look to our church's namesake—to God, the Trinity—to find a way of unity in diversity and diversity within unity, a way of reciprocity and mutuality. The Trinity tells us that even God is part of a team.

Pastoring a church named for the Trinity naturally prompts one to consider who and what the Trinity is—and there is no lack of material from others on the quest. My own understanding of the Trinity was revolutionized when I lived in Argentina and read Latin American theologians, especially Leonardo Boff, who contrasted the egalitarian, communal nature of the Trinity with the dictatorship of one tyrant at the top. Boff was familiar with fascism in Argentina and neighboring Chile, where one person wanted to hoard power rather than share it, to exercise sole control over all aspects of life and to govern alone. But the Trinity shows us that God takes a different approach to ruling. Yes, God is our sovereign, but God is not a solo tyrant. God is, in God's very being, a community, and knowing that divine identity guides the work of those who are made in God's image. As Boff put it:

> Believing in the Trinity means that truth is on the side of communion rather than exclusion; consensus translates truth better than imposi-

> tion; the participation of many is better than the dictate of a single one. . . . No one comes first and no one later, no one is superior or inferior. They are equally eternal, infinite, and merciful; they make up eternal community. . . . Community comes from this radical communion.

Christians often say that everyone is made in the image of God. Indeed, we say that so often that it sometimes sounds like a cliché—a slogan that's lost its force. A more unexpected way to say the exact same thing is this: We are made in the image of the Trinity. We are born bearing the image of the triune God and we are incorporated into the life of the Trinity through baptism. That's exactly why we baptize not just in the name of "God," but in the name of the Father and of the Son and of the Holy Spirit. The Bible gives us many names for God, and we use many other words (including female and non-gendered names) to speak about God in worship, but we always invoke the Trinity when we pray prayers about incorporating people more fully into the community—the prayers we pray when we baptize, confirm, and welcome new church members. We confess God as community when we pray about our human community, which we hope will pattern itself after the triune God. In the words of theologian Catherine Mowry LaCugna, "Mutuality rooted in communion among persons is a non-negotiable truth about our existence, the highest value and ideal of the Christian life, because for God mutual love among persons is supreme."

Baptism is always birth into a global, multiethnic, multicultural, multilingual community. Here at Trinity our congregational composition makes this nonnegotiable truth quite obvious and visible. It challenges us to grow toward our identity of trinitarian unity that refuses to downplay differences and moves us beyond coexistence to mutual respect and love. As Boff put it in the book I read so many years ago in Argentina,

> When the church forgets the source that gives it birth—the communion of the three divine Persons—it allows its unity to become uniformity; it lets one group of believers by itself assume all responsibilities, keeping others from participating; it allows its confessional interests to prevail over the interests of the reign; in short the river of bright waters is in danger of becoming a stagnant pool. We must be converted to the Trinity to recover diversity and communion, which create the dynamic unity that is ever open to new enrichment.

On Trinity Sunday, as part of our eucharistic liturgy, the pastor prays:

> You reveal your glory
> as the glory of the Father, the Son, and the Holy Spirit:
> equal in majesty, undivided in splendor, one Lord, one God,
> ever to be adored in your eternal glory.

Here in twenty-first-century New York, the vision of eternal glory is still to come; but the inner-workings of the Trinity, where mutual love overcomes every division, are revealed in glimpses day by day.

The day before Trinity Sunday, Marco walked into church at four in the afternoon for our Saturday confirmation class that he knew ended hours earlier. "Sorry, I'm late," he managed to tell me, which seemed odd until I looked up and saw his red face and body shivering with fury. I had met Marco, his baby brother Bling Bling, and their parents a few years earlier when they moved into the Frederick Douglass projects across the street. It was Family Day at Douglass Houses and I walked around greeting people, sampling offerings of potato salad and standing in line for hot dogs. Liliana saw my clerical collar and motioned me over. She wanted me to bless Bling Bling. I invited the family to church, and they showed up the next Sunday. I had no acolytes around to assist, so I asked Marco if he would like to light the candles. He nodded exuberantly, and Liliana filmed the event on her phone. Before long, Marco became a regular acolyte, and he and Bling Bling were baptized.

Over time I learned that they had moved to the neighborhood from a shelter where they'd lived after their home in Queens burned to the ground. I also learned that Marco's homelife still raged with other fires that flared between his parents. Eventually, his mother kicked his father out of the apartment: "I ripped off his penis ring and put it on my keychain. There was so much hair, I could make extensions from it . . . I took his bull for all the years, being shitted on in front of his crack whores; now from a white shirt, I gave him a red one." Marco was in the living room as Liliana told me this. He hugged her and said, "Mommy, I'm so proud of you. May I play hooky and we'll celebrate?" Then a day came that Marco called me from his home with his baby brother to tell me that their mother had locked herself in the bathroom with a knife and was threatening to kill herself.

Now Marco was late for confirmation class, asking to sit in the sanctuary, telling me that he came because he was afraid he would kill someone or something or himself if he didn't go to church. At his request, I left him alone in the sanctuary. After a while I got up to check on him. He told me about the cause of his fury, a group of boys who jumped him and took his baseball cap. My first thought was that this was not so bad and he was lucky nothing worse happened, but Marco started trembling again and crying. His grandmother had given him that hat. After the fire, that gift was the only physical object tying him to the woman who represented all the stability he'd ever known, a sanctuary lost upon her death. I didn't expect to go home later that day and hear a similar, plaintive cry from my mother.

When my mother's progressing Parkinson's made it impossible for her to live on her own, she moved in with us. Our already overcrowded home became even more tight as we tried to surround her with familiar objects, including hundreds of cookbooks. We installed shelving for them in the kitchen where they sat with their straight spines, daily reminders of my failure to maintain even moderate cooking standards, never mind emulating my mother's gourmet meals. The books showed up with an entourage of culinary paraphernalia, crowding our counters, standing at the ready to assist my mother in the cooking she insisted she would do for us. At first, we shared her sweet delusion. We stowed her carefully folded linens under the bed, yards of beautiful, heirloom linens for imaginary dinners in our nonexistent dining room, which now served as her bedroom.

On the day that Marco's hat was stolen, I came home to find her sitting in the kitchen with a box in her hands, her face ashen. "It's ruined," she said, and began to weep. She held a biscuit box for Ivins Sweet Marie Biscuits, bought and saved by my great-grandmother. It had sat in my mother's kitchen when she was a child and her grandmother lived with her. A piece of tape affixed to the tin, which bore my great-grandmother's handwriting, read, "Twine." Gregorio was cleaning the kitchen when he noticed the brittle, yellowed tape and helpfully scraped it off, sending five spidery letters down the drain. Those letters had tied my mother to so much that she had lost and was losing with every passing day. The scrubbed tin box became, at that moment, the epicenter of my mother's losses. It also illuminated our own inadequate efforts as caretakers, trying to hold it all together and often failing miserably.

My mother planned to join the church the following day and I still needed to finish my sermon. Some weeks, the sermon just needed a bit of final polishing on Saturday, but this week I was still struggling with the heart of the sermon—struggling to know how to preach on the Trinity. And, of course, I had not counted on devoting extra time to Marco and now to my mother, time subtracted from my sermon writing.

Finally seated at my desk, I tried to clear my mind and took a moment to grow quiet. I reconsidered the Scriptures that I would read in church the next morning. As I sat, a Hasidic tale came to mind. It tells of the pupil who asked his rabbi about the meaning of community one evening while he and other disciples sat around a fireplace. The rabbi sat in silence while the fire died down to a pile of glowing coals. Then he got up and took one coal out from the pile and set it apart on the stone hearth. Its fire and warmth soon died out. Community is everything—light, life, and fire of love. The divine identity traced on our souls that can never be stolen or scraped off.

My mother had been a church member in Summit, New Jersey, since I was a baby. Now she was going to become an official member of Trinity because this was where she would stay until she joined the church triumphant. We began preparations the night before, since I knew I would have no extra time in the morning. I helped her bathe. I showed Ana the red suit and asked her to help Oma get dressed. My mother woke up at six to get ready for eleven o'clock worship. She had actually been up since four but had "been good," as she put it, so that I could sleep. Many mornings she could not walk and had breakfast upstairs, but this morning, she walked downstairs to eat. At 9:30 a.m., Gregorio called me. My mother was sobbing and certain she would not be ready in time. I told her that Ana was taking a shower and there was still plenty of time to get dressed and get to church. It was a team effort.

We'd welcomed new members the previous week on Pentecost but my mother was not well enough that day. Today Trinity would receive two new members: my mother and Lucely, who was from the Dominican Republic. Lucely's first and only love had left her when she became pregnant with his child. When her daughter was two years old, he came back into her life and she became pregnant again. Same scenario. When her daughters were two and four, they both contracted meningitis and the younger one died. When Lucely sat in my office weeping and telling me this story, forty years had passed. For forty years, she had blamed herself for her daughter's death, her punishment for being young and in love and making the same mistake twice. She kept repeating "twice" with the weight of a judge's hammer. She felt the burden of racism and class too and asked me if my mother would mind standing next to her when they joined the church. Her question cut into the privilege I wear so often without thinking. Not only won't my mother mind; she will be pleased to have company.

When it was time to come forward, Ana walked with my mother, holding one of her hands. Lucely clasped my mother's other hand, blinking back tears. My mother wore her red suit with gold buttons, and Lucely wore a pink dress accented with a turquoise and gold scarf. Ana wore jeans and a Ramones T-shirt. As a church body we rejected evil and recited our trinitarian faith using the threefold Apostles' Creed. I always emphasize that this is something the whole congregation does together, not only those joining the church. Rejecting evil and holding on to faith is best done, is really only done, in community. On any given Sunday there will be some who can't muster any conviction, but they can lean on the faith of others. Blessedly, we are not all up or down on the same week.

I asked Lucely, "Will you strive for peace and justice in all the earth?" Then I asked my mother. "I will with the help of God," she answered. Our seminarian had to step in because my voice stopped working. My mother could not go to the toilet alone and yet she was standing up to strive for peace and justice. I cried because what I do is because of her. I cried because just getting here to stand up and speak those words had required so much of her. But here she stood, speaking up and holding on for dear life to Ana and to Lucely, who was now smiling. Marco sat nearby in his acolyte robes as I took in the holy work of the Trinity, pulling the threads of our lives together, as Boff describes it:

> present in time under shadows and crosses, at the end of time in the form of full openness and unending celebration . . . so close that we do not perceive it, so transcendent that it overflows us on all sides, so intimate that it dwells in the depths of our hearts, so real that it persists, despite sin and all its perverse consequences.

We sang our final hymn and went downstairs for some Tres Leches Cake, the perfect confection for Trinity Sunday. To make it, a vanilla sponge cake is soaked in three kinds of milk: evaporated milk, condensed milk, and heavy cream, creating one delicious treat. I sometimes marvel at the rich communities I've been placed in. I married a man who grew up in another country, picking cotton and sugarcane while I went to elementary school in the suburbs of New Jersey. I am a grandmother to Mia, who is half Ashkenazi Jew through my daughter-in-law and a mix of El Salvadoran and Tongan thanks to a sperm donor, making her one hundred percent the best thing in my life. As a straight, cisgender woman, I get to receive a generous, ongoing education from queer youth and drag queens. As a white woman often in nonwhite spaces, I have my privilege held before me in excruciatingly clear and needful ways. As anyone who lives in any sort of community—any marriage, any friendship—knows, authentic intimacy amid difference is, to say the least, challenging. It is perhaps the most elemental challenge of human sociability. Each Trinity Sunday, I remember that we can pursue this community not because such community is what God wants, but because such community is who God is—three-in-one, a community where difference never leads to violence, but love.

Ordinary Time

16

Numbers

> I turn on one of the networks, and they show an empty field. . . . I'm like, wait a minute. I made a speech. I looked out, the field was, it looked like a million, million and a half people.

The president's obsession with numbers, especially inflated numbers, became evident immediately following his inauguration. He and his press secretary, Sean Spicer, insisted, repeatedly, that the event drew the largest numbers ever, despite contrary evidence. Even in moments when one might expect the presidential focus to be elsewhere, such as while visiting Texas communities devastated by Hurricane Harvey, Trump's eyes were aglisten with the numbers: "What a crowd, what a turnout!" Honestly, this is one area where I identify with Trump. Pastors are conditioned to be obsessed with numbers too. We have to turn in annual reports—filled with numbers. How many baptisms? How many confirmations? How many people in the pews each Sunday? How many people under thirty? Over sixty? Children? Then we move to the financial figures: How many dollars pledged this year? Given? Spent? For the church—and for Trump—numbers determine survival, tempting us to massage the numbers a bit. If nobody records a count on some weeks, then I'll just estimate—and perhaps my memory will swell the ranks. Should a very pregnant woman count as one person or two? Hopefully the usher didn't count early in the service, since maybe thirty-five people rolled in late. I won't go into the invisible presence of the communion of saints who surround us—but I have considered them. They are here and their presence definitely counts in my book. Fortunately, I don't believe Trump knows about this particular group. In any case, I'm hardly in a position to judge his preoccupation with numbers.

Numbers will be in the news more than ever thanks to the 2020 Census. Even before the count begins, there's been contention about the process and the census documents. Under Obama, several federal agencies, including the Department of Justice, asked the Census Bureau to include questions about sexual orientation and gender identity. Soon after Trump took office, the questions were removed, and no amount of outcry or pressure from LGBTQIA+ activists has changed that. Advocacy groups need the numbers that the census could collect in lobbying for vital resources. Statistics about the queer community bear on statewide organizations and local community centers' planning. For instance, staff at senior centers may need training to understand the unique issues experienced by older, queer adults. Programming for youth may need to include a support group for queer teens. Some are concerned that a significant number of queer people will shun the census altogether because they feel their identity has been erased—and an artificially low count of people in any given town or state would have a negative impact on everyone who lives there, not only the queer population. Finally, it is easier to minimize the presence of LGBTQIA+ persons in our nation if we have no real numbers available. Queer people need to be counted as such so they can be seen and known as such.

Indeed, Trump has tried to erase LGBTQIA+ people not only from census records. Just two months after his inauguration, Trump sought to remove data on LGBTQIA+ persons from the National Survey of Older Americans Act Participants. This is an annual survey of those who receive services—nutritional services, senior centers, and transportation—through the Older Americans Act. Queer older adults face systemic discrimination resulting in disproportionate levels of economic insecurity and social isolation. Data on program participants can help illuminate how these safety-net programs serve—or fail to serve—this vulnerable population. Such data was collected and used since 2014 but is no longer part of the survey.

Similarly, the Department of Justice has sought to raise the age of crime victims (from sixteen to eighteen) who can be asked if they have been a victim due to sexual orientation or gender identity. This is a voluntary question—no young person is forced to disclose anything they wish to keep private—but in the past, many have chosen to reveal that they were targeted for reasons of sexual orientation or because they are transgender. I know this to be true from young people in Trinity's shelter. Those of us who wish to support queer teens who have been targeted in criminal attacks, and those who wish to reduce the frequency of such attacks, need these numbers.

Secretary of Education Betsy DeVos has removed questions related to gender expression or sexual orientation from the data collection about students who are bullied in public schools. Instead, such incidents all come under "bullying based on sex stereotyping." Eliza

Byard, who worked for years to get the Department of Education to have the agency count incidents of bullying because of perceived sexual orientation or gender expression, says, "For people who don't want to act on these issues, they don't want to see the problem, and it (has) the effect of erasing specific incidents at the top level of our data collection."

These numbers are essential to improving policies and protections for the queer community, but Trump has no interest in this count. He is, however, eager to count undocumented immigrants. The courts have now determined that the federal government cannot legally ask people whether they are US citizens as part of the 2020 census, much to Trump's displeasure. While queer people worry about not being counted, many immigrants are afraid of the count. Federal law states that individual data from the census cannot be shared with other governmental agencies (and therefore cannot be used to track people down for deportation), but that law has been circumvented before. Such data helped the government round up and imprison Japanese Americans in World War II. What reason have people to trust that something similar will not happen again? Undocumented immigrants may choose to avoid the census, and their numbers will be unknown as well.

Those who live in precarious housing situations also sometimes wish to evade the census, for fear of calling attention to their questionable domiciliary arrangements and thus becoming homeless. People who live in public housing may open their doors to family members or friends in urgent need of housing, even though those relatives are not on the lease. What might begin as a temporary visit can become permanent, and the additional residents can eventually lead to the leaseholder's eviction. Those who live in an apartment and use a Section 8 housing voucher are allowed to host a guest for only fourteen consecutive days and no more than twenty-one nights total in any one year. These rules even apply to close relatives such as a parent, sibling, child, or grandchild if they were not part of the original household upon application. A person found guilty of housing others without permission can be legally accused of fraud and lose not only their housing but also the option for a future Section 8 voucher. All of this provides reason enough to make people in such situations leery of the census.

Of course, many people who live in precarious housing arrangements are immigrants. When I was new to Trinity, I walked around my new neighborhood and wondered where the Mexican immigrants lived. Most of the housing options I noticed—public housing, rent-stabilized apartments, and pricy condos—seemed unlikely. I found my answer a few months later, that first July, when I went to visit the families of the children who attended our summer camp. One address was less than a block from the church. It was a large building that rented rooms to tourists on some floors and to families on others. The accommodations seemed fine for the tourists, who spent virtually no time cooped up in their little rooms, but it was altogether different for those who made a home there. When I visited the Ramirez family, I stepped into a nine-by-nine-foot room with a bunk bed, dresser, chair, and little table. The parents slept on the bottom bunk and their two daughters shared the top. They didn't have a kitchen. Many families used a communal bathroom in the hall. Juana and Carlos endured the challenges of this small living space because it enabled their girls to attend better schools than those in neighborhoods with cheaper rents.

One daughter, Valeria, has now graduated from college and works in cutting-edge digital-marketing research. She serves as our congregation's president and is a DACA recipient. (Deferred Action for Childhood Arrivals allows some brought into the country as children to receive a renewable two-year period of deferred action from deportation, allowing them to work and study.) Valeria also makes time to mentor other DACA Dreamers in navigating college admissions and job searches. Her younger sister, Verónica, received a full scholarship to a prestigious college. She celebrates her roots through intricate twirls of indigenous Mexican dances and reaching out through Cosecha, an immigrant rights organization. Recently, Juana brought Verónica to my office for a blessing before she left for a semester in Mexico. Juana also brought me a gift from her mother, Lupe, back in Puebla: a gorgeous, hand-embroidered altar cloth with an image of the Virgin of Guadalupe surrounded by roses. I called Lupe to express my gratitude. Listening to her voice across the miles, giving thanks for the faith and circumstances that have brought us together, the border disappeared.

That first summer, my next visit to a camper's family took me to the kind of classic Upper West Side prewar building that filmmakers love. I couldn't figure out how our day-camp family could afford it. The doorman was unfamiliar with the family I sought, which confirmed my first thought—I'd written down the wrong address. I returned to church, and the next day, found the camper's mom to confirm the address. She insisted I'd gone to the correct building. Later that afternoon, when she picked up her children, I went home with them.

The super had carved out a bonus for himself by illegally renting space in the boiler room. Getting into the makeshift living space required descending a steep stairway meant for boiler maintenance, not for families with small children lugging groceries, laundry, and strollers. The only way in, or out, was through a thick, fireproof door that was required to remain closed at all times. It was July, but despite the oppressive heat outside and lack of ventilation inside, the space stayed relatively cool, a singular advantage to living underground. The mother offered cold, orange soda from the jury-rigged refrigerator and the children, suddenly shy, pointed to their colorful assortment of day-camp artwork on a dresser. Upstairs, the tenants enjoyed airy, ornamented apartments with high ceilings, large windows, herringbone wooden floors, vintage brass fixtures, and wide hallways. On the other hand, the Virgin of Guadalupe had a place of honor on the wall of the boiler room.

City law says that all living spaces must have windows and that all cellar dwellings are illegal, but when you have no other options, you make do. A *New York Times* article, "Underground Lives: The Sunless Lives of Immigrants in Queens," describes the plight of thousands of people who live in a shadow city away from public sight. Countless families like these are part of the fabric of our nation, doing jobs that others decline to do, but they are not likely to be counted in the census.

The church counts fifty-two Sundays in a year. Many fall in special holiday seasons: the fifty days of Eastertide, the twelve days of Christmas, the weeks of Epiphany. But many weeks, many Sundays—those stretching between Pentecost and Advent—are part of no special festival. These days fall in what we call Ordinary Time, not because the days lack all splendor but because, not being linked to a special season, we simply count them. "Ordinary" here means not "typical," but "pertaining to ordinal numbers," those numbers (first, second, third) that designate something's place in a series. So the Sundays of Ordinary Time are those Sundays we count, rather than those Sundays we decorate with festival names. You can count between eighteen to twenty-three such Sundays depending on when Easter falls in any given year.

My earliest memories include watching the play of seasons on the trees outside my bedroom window—feathery, pale-green buds in spring; the lush, deep-green leaves of summer; the autumn reds and golds with a morning sheen of silver dew; and winter's black, snow-lined branches. Having lived most of my life in the Northeast, I've always loved the changing seasons outside my windows—and inside the church as well. Inside, a different round of seasons unfolds each year, also with colors—the blues of Advent, purple during Lent, gold for Easter, flaming red for Pentecost, and the greens of Ordinary Time. Just as I could look out my window and instantly know the season, I could enter the sanctuary and know what church season we were in because we change the color of the linens that hang from our church furniture (the altar, the pulpit) for different liturgical seasons.

The musical *Rent*'s "Seasons of Love" begins by asking how to measure a year with "five hundred twenty-five thousand six hundred minutes." The church year proposes that the minutes, days, and years of our lives are measured not only in sunsets, midnights, and cups of coffee, but in seasons of divine love, marking the birth, life, death, and resurrection of Jesus, the coming of the Holy Spirit, and other special days of grace. These seasons were as much a part of my life growing up as the seasons outside my window, but I understand that is not true for many people.

To teach about the seasons, I've taken fifty-two pieces of construction paper in the various liturgical colors and put them in an oval on the floor so we could walk through the year of Sundays and talk about the meanings of the different days and seasons. The longest part of our walk is always Ordinary Time, where we count out the weeks we measure telling stories. On each Sunday of the year, Christians read Scripture in church. Trinity, like many churches, follows the ancient pattern of Scripture reading known as a lectionary—that is, I don't decide what passages of the Bible we'll hear each Sunday; I follow a table that tells me that on the eleventh Sunday of Ordinary Time, we will read Isaiah 58:9–14 and on the twenty-third Sunday of Ordinary Time we will read Luke 21:5–19.

Of course, many readings are left out of the lectionary, and thus never heard in church on Sundays. Some of these overlooked readings have much in common with the overlooked people whom our census will not count; both deserve to come out into the light. One of my favorites of these overlooked readings comes from the book of Numbers. Numbers gets its name from the census God orders Moses to take in the second verse of the book, and census numbers thread throughout. The passage I especially love comes from chapters 26 and 27, chapters that bring us to a decisive point in the lives of the Israelite tribes, who've been making their way through the wilderness since leaving their enslavement in Egypt. They now stand on the plains of Moab, with their destination ahead of them, on the other side of the Jordan River.

When the sojourners face the challenge of reorganizing for life across the Jordan River, they begin by taking a census, the second census described in Numbers. In addition to numbers, the census includes names. Each of the twelve tribes of Israel is named and each tribe has three to six clans with their own named heads, about sixty of them. The Bible gives the total figures for each tribe and if you add them up, the Numbers' census counts 601,730 people, none of them named besides the tribal and clan heads.

But the group gathered on the plains of Moab is much bigger because the census did not include women and children. The first purpose of the census was to determine battle readiness. Only those who were seen as fit to fight battles were counted, and that left out the women and children. The second purpose of the census was to determine how to distribute the land. Larger clans needed more land and smaller clans needed less. Property rights were passed on through males of each clan.

In the context of the book of Numbers, the invisibility of women and children in the census is not surprising. What is astonishing is what you find as you move through the list of tribes in Numbers 26 and come to the eighth tribe, the tribe of Manasseh: "The descendants of Manasseh: of Machir, the clan of the Machirites; and Machir was the father of Gilead; of Gilead, the clan of the Gileadites" (Num. 26:29), and on and on until you hit verse 33: "Now Zelophehad son of Hepher had no sons, but daughters: and the names of the daughters of Zelophehad were Mahlah, Noah, Hoglah, Milcah, and Tirzah." It's not remarkable that women are excluded from the census. It's remarkable that five women are in fact named in the census.

And not only are they named; their speech is recorded:

> They stood before Moses, Eleazar the priest, the leaders, and all the congregation, at the entrance of the tent of meeting, and they said, "Our father died in the wilderness; he was not among the company of those who gathered themselves together against the Lord in the company of Korah, but died for his own sin; and he had no sons. Why should the name of our father be taken away from his clan because he had no son? Give to us a possession among our father's brothers." (Numbers 27:2-4)

Zelophehad had died on the sojourn in the wilderness. The five sisters had no brothers, husbands, or in-laws, and therefore no rights to any land. They stood together with their people on the edge of the wilderness, but the census made clear that they didn't count for anything. When everyone crossed over, they would remain forever on the far edge, disconnected from power, from land, and from life.

While the rest of the group mobilized itself through the census to determine critical mass for battles on the other side of the Jordan, the five sisters saw a battle to fight right where they stood, within their own community. And the battle came with real risk. Would "Moses, Eleazar the priest, the leaders, and the whole assembly" hear, really hear, the justice of their claim? As vulnerable women without men, they had the most to lose if the community rejected them—and rejection was quite likely if they agitated the leadership. Moses's own sister Miriam had been censured earlier for daring to question her brother's position as spokesperson and community advocate. In reaction to Miriam's outspoken questioning—her suggestion that she and her brother Aaron should also have leadership roles in the community—she became covered with leprosy and had to be shut away for a week in order to learn her lesson. (Notably, Aaron had joined Miriam in her questioning, but he was not turned leprous.) This was not an encouraging example for Mahlah, Noah, Hoglah, Milcah, and Tirzah. But these five sisters spoke out anyway.

It would have been much less risky to approach Moses in private and plead with him to work out some special deal for them, but they understand that their well-being is connected to the well-being of others, so they make their case in public, as a witness and inspiration to others.

> Moses brought their case before the LORD. And the LORD spoke to Moses, saying: The daughters of Zelophehad are right in what they

> are saying; you shall indeed let them possess an inheritance among their father's brothers and pass the inheritance of their father on to them. . . . It shall be for the Israelites a statute and ordinance, as the Lord commanded Moses. (Num. 27:5–7, 11b)

Because Mahlah, Noah, Hoglah, Milcah, and Tirzah present their petition to Moses in public, their individual case serves to change the Israelite inheritance law to include women. These sisters filed one of the earliest lawsuits on record. In fact, this case is one of the oldest still cited as an authority. As recently as 1924, the *American Bar Association Journal* cites Numbers 27, describing Mahlah, Noah, Hoglah, Milcah, and Tirzah's win as "an early declaratory judgment in which the property rights of women are clearly set forth."

For Mahlah, Noah, Hoglah, Milcah, and Tirzah, census-taking turned into an opportunity for power, for the redistribution of wealth, and the empowerment of women. There have been times in American history when it's been clear that the census potentially could be used similarly—or used to minimize and disregard those on the margins. (That's why, to take just one example, there were heated debates in 1930 about how well the census counted the unemployed; a well-executed census could show just how serious of a problem unemployment was, and where unemployment was concentrated, and thus imply responses that business and government might be compelled to offer.) Counting, as Donald Trump understands, is never neutral.

I don't think it's any coincidence that, as the Gospel of Luke tells us, Jesus was born during a census. God came to earth not only in a manger; God came to earth during the season of counting. Every time I read a newspaper article about the census, every time I hear the president on the news inflating his numbers, I am reminded that we can put our own counting toward various ends. For women, for the dispossessed, for immigrants, for the precariously housed, for queer people, for all of us, our counting can advance, or it can prevent, the kind of community Jesus always seeks. My parents taught me to count with an abacus filled with brightly colored beads. I'm doing the same with Mia, teaching her not to skip over any of them.

17

Autumnal Saints

> I believe that there's a change in weather and I think it changes both ways.

Throughout the year, the church devotes a number of days to celebrating saints—people the church believes have lived especially holy lives: third-century martyrs Perpetua and Felicity on March 7; twelfth-century Benedictine nun Hildegard of Bingen on September 17 (a Christian mystic, composer, poet, scientist, physician, and herbalist); Bartolomé de las Casas on July 18 (a Dominican missionary who wrote to expose the oppression and torture of indigenous peoples by Europeans in the Americas and to call for the abolition of slavery there). Not all saints are centuries old, of course, or famous for overtly churchy accomplishments: Florence Nightingale's saint's day is August 13.

We Lutherans don't believe that saints were perfect people. In the Bible, when St. Paul writes letters to young churches, he addresses his letter to "the saints in Rome" or to "the saints in Corinth," and reading the letters makes it clear that these saints were not sinless people, nor was

St. Paul. In these letters, "saints" refers to people beloved of God, people who belong to God, though they are flawed. We are all sinners and saints.

But we do recognize that some people lived with singular holiness; despite their failings, we can learn from their faith and from the shape of their lives. Some of these saints are hidden to all but a handful—every church has their own local list, and every person may have their own private list—but others are known to millions. On All Saints' Sunday, many churches remember those who have died, especially those most dear to us. For All Saints' at Trinity, we cover the altar with a white cloth and have a bowl of markers for people to write the names of their deceased loved ones on the altar cloth. We do this to remember that the communion of saints is present with us as we celebrate Holy Communion.

All Saints' Sunday falls on the first Sunday in November, the same day as the New York City marathon. This convergence strikes me as sheer serendipity. On All Saints' Sunday we hear a reading from the book of Hebrews: "Therefore, since we are surrounded by so great a cloud of witnesses, let us also lay aside every weight and the sin that clings so closely, and let us run with perseverance the race that is set before us" (Heb. 12:1). I like to think that the saints who have already crossed the finish line of their lives remain close to us, behind sight, cheering us on our way. At Trinity, we also try to lift up saints from this cloud of witnesses throughout the year—including queer saints, African American saints, female saints, Latinx saints, and every autumn, our calendar gives us a trio of widely known saints—St. Francis (October 3), St. Luke (October 18), and St. Martin of Tours (November 11).

St. Francis is, perhaps, one of the most popular saints. Many places around the neighborhood do not allow people to hang signs with any religious content, like the local library that understandably must remain nonpartisan—except when it comes to St. Francis. I cannot post invitations for neighbors to attend Sunday worship; however, even the library will make an exception if my flyers invite people to accompany their pets for a blessing as we celebrate St. Francis. The library happily promotes the blessing of pets, just not people. We can hang flyers everywhere for St. Francis, but not for St. Luke or St. Martin or any other saint I can think of. Francis is such a favorite, I think, because he was known to love animals (birds and wolves were said to listen to him when he preached), to care about ecology, and to pursue peace. "Lord, make me an instrument of your peace," runs a prayer attributed to St. Francis. "Where there is hatred, let me sow love; . . . Where there is despair, hope; . . . Grant that I may not so much seek, to be consoled, as to console. . . . For it is in giving that we receive." Francis has wide fandom.

As a patron saint for the environment, the one place that may not welcome Francis is the White House. As a first-round presidential candidate, Trump dismissed climate change as a "hoax" invented by the Chinese. After becoming president, he picked Scott Pruitt—a man who rejects the role of carbon dioxide in climate change and has stated that if the planet does warm, it may "help humans flourish"—to head the Environmental Protection Agency. Under Pruitt, EPA scientists were not permitted to share any scientific findings related to climate change with the public; all such data was for internal use only. One scientist at the EPA wrote:

> The constant attacks on science and facts by the current administration has negatively impacted scientists in the agency. Effects range from anger and frustration to depression and even opting to retire early. Twenty-five years of experience with 3 federal agencies and I've never seen anything like this—it is appalling.

So, when planning our annual St. Francis celebration, it seemed like a good idea to highlight Francis's care for the earth—and to include our resident scientist in the planning. Emily took out time, in the final days of preparing her PhD defense, to write "The Scientist's Lament" for our liturgy. On the day of the celebration, we blessed animals outside, invited everyone (including pets) inside, and began worship with Emily's lament, which reads in part:

> You might have heard of the panda, the gorilla, leopard, the emperor penguin, the manatee, the rhino. But have you heard that 26,000 species are threatened with extinction?
>
> Have you heard that 41% of insects have declined in just ten years, and at the current rate, none will be left at all in a century? Birds will starve, lizards will starve, fish will starve. . . .
>
> Have you heard that 3 billion birds have disappeared from North American skies over the past 50 years? 30% of birds are already gone.

We'd hung a dozen, colorful, cardboard birds from strings between the columns in front of the altar. As Emily read, another congregant stepped forward with scissors and cut the birds so that they slowly fell, one by one, to the floor around the altar. As they fell, I realized that we had made a mistake printing out the Scientist's Lament because many people had their heads down reading along as Emily spoke, not noticing the falling birds. Still, one person commented later that it shocked her to look up and see that the birds were no longer there, and then to notice them lying lifeless around the altar.

Two weeks later, St. Luke's Day arrived. Luke wrote one of the four Gospels. Because St. Paul mentions, in his letter to the Colossians, that Luke is a physician, we associate him with medicine and healing. The hospital ten blocks from Trinity is onc of many hospitals named St. Luke's. We commemorate St. Luke on the Sunday closest to his feast day with a healing service. In place of the sermon, I give a brief introduction to healing prayer and to St. Luke and then the people walk around the church, reflect, and pray at any (or all) of ten healing stations that have been set up. We always provide an opportunity for the laying on of hands and anointing with oil; for placing votive candles on a map of the nations one wishes to pray for; for attaching sticky prayer notes to a cross. Popular with children, but open to all ages, is a table with supplies to make cards for the sick. Outside the main doors, we hold a space to pray for those who have been hurt by the church and do not feel safe entering, and for those who are incarcerated.

Other stations vary from year to year, depending on current events in the world and the preoccupations of the seminarians who help create the stations. Last year, our seminary fieldwork student, Alyssa, set up a station to help people consider what healing in relationship to disability means. The station explained ableism and included helpful information to guide people in considering ways they might heal the harm caused by discrimination against people with disabilities.

In light of the escalation in murders of trans women of color, we covered a large cardboard cross with the now-dead women's photos and names, twenty at the time of this writing in 2019. The cross stood next to an angel who held a bowl filled with slips of paper, each bearing these words from Psalm 139: "I praise you God for I am awesomely and wonderfully made." Parishioner after parishioner stood before the cross and offered these words for themselves, and for the twenty dead.

In 2020, St. Luke's Day arrives a few weeks before the election. Our denomination has joined others in signing on to something called Golden Rule 2020, which invites us to pray for the healing of divisions in our country and reads in part:

> We are Christians with different theological and political views who have come together to express concern about the polarization and incivility that is tearing our country apart. We are also deeply troubled by the prospect of an angry and hateful political campaign season in 2020 that will further divide us as a nation. We believe that we can find guidance through this national dilemma in the teachings of Jesus. In particular, we believe that Jesus' command to "do unto others as you would have them do unto you" should be taken seriously by Christians who engage in political activity. We also believe that if enough people follow this "Golden Rule" principle, it will help generate the respect and civility we so desperately need in our country.

What kind of healing station might we create? I long for healing of divisions but personally find the Golden Rule 2020 effort misguided. To my mind, we desperately need not to generate civility but to overcome injustice and to relieve suffering—even though doing so might lead to increasing polarization. When the Trump Administration has held nearly seventy thousand children in detention facilities, civility is not what's called for.

Martin Luther King Jr. heard a similar call for civility, demanding that he tone down his rhetoric and activism. I'd love to see the day when his response from the Birmingham City Jail has lost its relevance, but I don't expect to live that long. In his letter to white moderate clergy, King answered the complaints of those who prefer "a negative peace which is the absence of tension to a positive peace which is the presence of justice."

> We merely bring to the surface the hidden tension that is already alive. We bring it out in the open, where it can be seen and dealt with. Like a boil that can never be cured so long as it is covered up but must be opened with all its ugliness to the natural medicines of air and light, injustice must be exposed, with all the tension its exposure creates, to the light of human conscience and the air of national opinion before it can be cured.

Perhaps our healing station will have a table spread with red cloth and blue cloth. We will place King's letter in the center and surround it with photos of the children who have died in detention centers and on the border. Or photos of lost trans women. Or photos of Black men and women, targeted for hate crimes more than any other group. "How long, O Lord?" we will cry with the prophets. "Come, Lord Jesus!" we will pray with the saints before us.

On November 11, we arrive at the feast day of St. Martin of Tours. Trinity was founded by German-born Americans; our baptismal font is engraved with the words *Lasset Die Kindlein Zu Mir Kommet*, "Let the Children Come to Me." But, like most people in our nation today, when I hear about "immigrants," I think of those who come from south of the border. In my first few years at Trinity, I assumed that though we might celebrate baptism in Spanish—or once in French—the parish's days of welcoming Germans were behind us. So I, the daughter of a German immigrant, was surprised when a few families whose jobs had taken them from Hamburg and Berlin to New York began to show up with their children in Wee Worship. Before long, I was doing baptisms in German.

Just as immigrants from south of our border bring their foods and customs, so have these German families, and one of the more delightful traditions they bring is St. Martin's Day. Martin of Tours lived in the fourth century. His father was a soldier in the Roman army and named Martin for Mars, the Roman god of war. Imperial law required a son to take up the profession of his father, but Martin had begun studying for baptism and had no desire to fight. Nonetheless, bowing to paternal pressure, Martin postponed baptism and entered the Roman army. He was a model solider, but he was not happy.

One day, his troops passed by a barely covered, poor beggar shivering in the winter cold. While his comrades rode on, Martin stopped his horse, took his sword, and cut his woolen cloak in two, wrapping the man in one half. That night, Martin saw Jesus in a dream dressed in the cloak. "Martin, who is not yet baptized, has clothed me," said Jesus. When Martin woke up, he was determined to be baptized and told his superior that he could not continue in his regiment. Martin was imprisoned, but after a relatively short sentence, he did finally receive the sacrament of baptism, and he became a monk. Martin became known for his preaching in the countryside around the monastery, and for his kindness and generosity.

The people wanted to make him their bishop, but Martin resisted, eventually having to hide from those who insistently sought after him. Supposedly, the noise of a gaggle of geese outside his hiding place led the people to him and he finally relented. He became the third bishop of Tours, served until his death in 397, and was buried on November 11. Germans celebrate with a goose dinner, and children prepare lanterns, processing through the streets in search of Martin. At the end, the children receive cones of candy.

At Trinity, we don't replicate the goose dinner, but we have enjoyed another German custom—baking and eating little St. Martin breads, which are like gingerbread men without the ginger. We've also introduced our own St. Martin's Day tradition, based on Martin's encounter with the beggar. Beginning around Halloween, we collect coats, blankets, hats, scarves, and gloves; before it grows too frightfully cold, we give them to the youth in our shelter and to those in need who attend our community Thanksgiving meal. But first, on the Sunday closest to November 11, we heap them around the altar in memory of St. Martin, whose kindness lives on here, as it might anywhere the baptized gather.

Christ the King Sunday

18

Crown Him with Tear Gas

Thank you to Wayne Allyn Root for the very nice words. "President Trump is . . . like he's the King of Israel . . . like he is the second coming of God."

I've never been a big fan of Christ the King Sunday. Not all churches celebrate it, and some years, I've wished that my denomination skipped it too. Of all the titles or names for Jesus, I do not favor King. With so many choices—Shepherd, Savior, Vine, Bread of Life, Light of the World, Mother Hen, Bright Morning Star—King doesn't speak to me. When I ask the young children in Wee Worship what they can tell me about kings, they're excited to share their knowledge—kings live in a castle; kings sit on a throne; kings wear a golden crown; and kings are rich. None of this relates to Jesus. It's anachronistic. At least, it was.

When Trump became president, I changed my mind about Christ the King Sunday. Before he moved to Washington, he lived in a $100 million, 24-karat-gold-encrusted penthouse in Trump Tower with a central space that looked like the throne room of a king—King Louis

XIV to be precise. The penthouse was intentionally decorated to look like a mini Palace of Versailles on Fifth Avenue. For someone who likes that kind of thing, the White House is quite a step down, but the matchless power makes up for it.

The Christian right likes to compare Trump to King Cyrus, who became the first king of Persia in the sixth century BCE. Cyrus, of course, was not Jewish, but the prophet Isaiah hails Cyrus for liberating the Jews from captivity in Babylon. In Isaiah, God declares, "I've called" Cyrus and I am "using him to do what I want with Babylon." The identification of Trump with Cyrus enables evangelicals to overlook Trump's apparent lack of evangelical piety since Cyrus was a nonbeliever anointed by God as an instrument of salvation for the Jews. The fact that Isaiah lifts up Cyrus in chapter 45 (never mind that our chapter divisions did not exist before the thirteenth century) and that Trump is the forty-fifth president of the United States makes this identification irrefutable. Trump himself was quick to Tweet the words of an off-kilter conspiracy theorist riffing on this theme:

> Thank you to Wayne Allyn Root for the very nice words. "President Trump is the greatest President for Jews and for Israel in the history of the world . . . and the Jewish people in Israel love him . . . like he's the King of Israel. They love him like he is the second coming of God."

Without using the royal title, Trump's lawyers imputed nondemocratic, kingly powers to the president during the impeachment hearings, insisting that he is not beholden to any checks and balances on his power as long as he's the seated president, on his royal throne, as it were. Trump himself makes no secret about his infatuation and envy of various dictators. These days cry out for Christ the King Sunday.

For churches that follow a calendar of liturgical seasons, Christ the King Sunday falls on the final Sunday of the church year, the Sunday before Advent, crowning the year. It's a relatively recent addition to the calendar that was introduced by Pope Pius XI in 1925 as the Solemnity of Our Lord Jesus Christ, King of the Universe. In 1925, in Italy, where the pope lived, Benito Mussolini, the leader of the National Fascist Party, had claimed that supremacy for himself. Over in Germany, also in 1925, Hitler had published his antisemitic manifesto, *Mein Kampf,* and rose in his bid for absolute power as the leader of the Nazi party. In light of these political developments, Pius XI decided to boldly assert that Jesus Christ is the one who reigns supreme and to remind Christians that their allegiance is to their spiritual ruler, Jesus Christ, as opposed to any earthly leader who claimed supremacy. Before long, several other denominations adopted Christ the King Sunday.

At Trinity, we have not done much to mark the day. It seems easier with children. During Wee Worship, I read the story of King Midas and then we talk about how Jesus is a different kind of king: "For where your treasure is, there your heart will be also." As a reminder that we are Jesus's treasure, all the children make their own crowns, heavy with glue and glitter. Last year, we read from John: "'You say that I am a king. For this I was born, and for this I came into the world, to testify to the truth. Everyone who belongs to the truth listens to my voice.' Pilate asked him, 'What is truth?'" We talked about truth-telling and that sometimes it's easy to tell the truth, but other times, it can be hard. Part of Jesus's power is that he always told the truth, even when it seemed like telling the truth was not going to work out well for him. We can ask Jesus to help us tell the truth too. This makes sense to children.

This year I'd like to do more. The assigned text is the story of Jesus crucified between two criminals. Perhaps, we'll fashion a crown of thorns out of barbed wire to call attention to his revolutionary kingdom. After worship, a young woman who works in criminal justice reform and prison abolition will lead a conversation about what's happening here with the impending closure of Rikers Island and the mayor's plan to build four borough-based jails and what alternatives to prisons and jails might look like.

With adults, the reign of Christ requires a complete reorientation no matter how we cast our vote. In Matthew's Gospel for Christ the King Sunday, even Jesus's closest followers, the righteous, fail to recognize him because his reign takes him so far from the conventional trappings of power. Jesus speaks of a final judgment where he will sit on his throne of glory, separating those who will inherit his kingdom from those who will not:

> for I was hungry and you gave me food, I was thirsty and you gave me something to drink, I was a stranger and you welcomed me, I was naked and you gave me clothing, I was sick and you took care of me, I was in prison and you visited me. (Matt. 25:35–36)

The righteous answer that they have never seen him in any of these debased circumstances "and the king will answer them, 'Truly I tell you, just as you did it to one of the least of these who are members of my family, you did it to me" (Matt. 25:40). For many Christians, Jesus's words here have been airbrushed with familiarity, but in reality they are shocking, and they put the church into direct conflict with the state.

On Christ the King Sunday of 2018, November 25, the United States Customs and Border Patrol closed all vehicle and pedestrian traffic at the San Ysidro port of entry between Tijuana and San Diego.

Border agents fired tear gas at refugees and asylum-seekers, including many children, in the vicinity of the border fence. The world saw photos of terrified children, still in diapers, trying to run away. In church, we heard news from a different throne "far above all rule and authority and power and dominion, and above every name that is named, not only in this age but also in the age to come" (Eph. 1:21). We heard the scandalous words of Christ the King: "I was a stranger and you did not welcome me" (Matt. 25:43).

ADVENT

19

Angelus Bells

I am your voice! To every parent who dreams for their child, and every child who dreams for their future, I say these words to you: *I'm With You, and I will FIGHT for you, and I will WIN for YOU.*

The Sundays of Advent, a four-week period before Christmas, begin with a different voice:

> A voice of one calling:
> "In the wilderness prepare
> the way for the LORD;
> make straight in the desert
> a highway for our God." (Isa. 40:3–5)

The season of Advent invites the church to head for a wilderness far from the corridors of power in order to more clearly hear the voice of God. During Advent, the church often pairs the prophet Isaiah's words with readings about Jesus's cousin, John the Baptist.

> In the fifteenth year of the reign of Emperor Tiberius, when Pontius Pilate was governor of Judea, and Herod was ruler of Galilee, and his brother Philip ruler of the region of Ituraea and Trachonitis, and Lysanias ruler of Abilene, during the high priesthood of Annas and Caiaphas, the word of God came to John son of Zechariah in the wilderness. (Luke 3:1-2)

At the head of this who's who list is Emperor Tiberius. The Roman senator and historian Tacitus describes this tyrant's murderous fit of rage upon discovering that his close associate and confidant, Sejanus, betrayed him in an attempt to seize power.

> Executions were now a stimulus to his fury, and he ordered the death of all who were lying in prison under accusation of complicity with Sejanus. There lay, singly or in heaps, the unnumbered dead, of every age and sex, the illustrious with the obscure. Kinsfolk and friends were not allowed to be near them, to weep over them, or even to gaze on them too long. Spies were set round them, who noted the sorrow of each mourner and followed the rotting corpses, till they were dragged to the Tiber, where, floating or driven on the bank, no one dared to burn or to touch them.

The fact that Tiberius was far from the most brutal of Roman emperors begins to explain the long history of tensions between church and state, from the early Christian refusal to reverence the emperor as a god to the defiant act of kneeling during the national anthem. Going down the list of dignitaries under Tiberius, we come to Pontius Pilate, the Roman governor who oversaw the fake trial and execution of Jesus. We also read about Philip, who married his niece Salome, younger by thirty-nine years, basically a child who was sexualized and blamed for the tragic death of John the Baptist, whose head was presented to Herod on a platter.

Three decades earlier, Herod completed one of his major construction projects: the restoration of the Jerusalem temple that was severely damaged in a series of wars. Raised as a Jew, now serving at the whim of Rome, Herod had a choice between building a sanctuary that honored his Jewish heritage or selling out for the perks, privileges, and pleasures that came from Roman colonization. Herod chose to design the baths of Jewish purification as almost indistinguishable from fashionable Roman baths, mirroring the architectural structures of Roman hedonism, oppression, and organized disdain for the poor and needy. In terrible irony, these *mikvoth*, or holy baths, morphed into a symbol of spiritual pollution and corruption, not unlike the baptismal pools of the prosperity gospel church. The shameless foundation of Herod's vast array of such construction projects prefigured the works of Robert Moses, Trump, and Extell.

John the Baptist was expected to serve in the Jerusalem temple since his father was a temple priest and his mother descended from a priestly family, but he departed for the wilderness instead, protesting the tyranny and dysfunction of Jerusalem's elite. It was also a return to his spiritual roots. The wilderness is where the Hebrew people journeyed in their exodus from slavery to freedom. The wilderness is where they learned to trust in God's mercy leading them toward an unfamiliar place of promise on the other side of the Jordan River. John calls the people out of Jerusalem to that same river as if to the waters of a true *mikvah*, or purification bath. According to Luke's Gospel, God skips over the long list of dignitaries to address John in the desert.

Three centuries later, after church and state joined forces under Emperor Constantine, the desert fathers and mothers followed the example of John. Twentieth-century Trappist monk Thomas Merton described these hermits as those "who did not believe in letting themselves be passively guided and ruled by a decadent state." They rejected "the false, formal self, fabricated under social compulsion 'in the world.' They sought a way to God that was uncharted and freely chosen, not inherited from others who had mapped it out beforehand." When I read Merton's words about "a false, formal self, fabricated under social compulsion," I also hear echoes of countless nonwhite colleagues in the church who have experienced the force of "ecclesial compulsion" and are refusing to conform to it, honoring their own divine inheritance.

For Merton, the path of the hermits, rejecting the rule of a decadent state that divided them from themselves, had powerful political implications that could not be more relevant today. From his own monastic cell, Merton could see that "the great travelers and colonizers of the Renaissance were, for the most part, men who perhaps were capable of the things they did precisely because they were alienated from themselves." With their steel Toledo swords and other weapons of conquest they imposed on others "their own confusion and alienation." This certainly gives us one way to interpret the inhumanity and tyranny of these days.

Any time can make a good time for a retreat, but each Advent I hear the invitation to listen with special attention for the voice of God who spoke to Isaiah and John in the wilderness, and that led me to a Benedictine monastery for some solitude and reflection. The heart of Benedictine spirituality is to welcome every guest as Christ, and I arrived in time for evening prayer. As in many monasteries, the monks ring a bell in the evening, calling the community to pray at what they believe is the hour the angel Gabriel appeared to greet Mary with tidings of inconceivable conception. It is called the angelus bell and some medieval bells are inscribed with the opening words of the angelus prayer: *Ave Maria. Gratia plena. Dominus tecum*, "Hail Mary, full of grace, the Lord is with you."

At the monastery, I heard the bells six times a day, calling monks and guests to common prayer. Despite the focus on indiscriminate hospitality, I'm not sure how Benedict would have felt about Dexter, the serial killer I smuggled in through Netflix on my iPhone. I went to the monastery to get away from distractions and to focus on prayer and writing. Mostly that is what I did, but this trip also counted as vacation time and I decided to permit myself several Dexter breaks. I have no explanation as to why I would find the escapades of a fictitious serial killer so thoroughly enjoyable and even relaxing. I felt guilty about watching Dexter slicing and dicing his victims in such a sacred space, but the guilt did not deter me. A group of Episcopalian priests were also at the monastery for a retreat on the art of hearing confessions. I shared mealtimes with them, but I did not mention Dexter.

Perhaps St. Anthony the Great, who moved to the desert in the third century, would have understood. Anthony is often depicted warding off temptations as assorted devils aim their knives and other sharp implements at him from every side. Artists have had the time of their lives inventing diabolical creatures to torture Anthony, my favorite being the devil lobster seen in a fifteenth-century illuminated

French manuscript. On the other hand, I sense it would be unwise to compare my attachment to Dexter with the trials of St. Anthony who never appears to be enjoying the experience and who is considered the father of Christian monasticism. Perhaps my assignations with Dexter make me more akin to the artists who definitely appear to enjoy the diversions provided by their perverse, imaginative forays. Happily, through no discipline of my own and despite my adventures with Dexter, I emerged from the Hudson Valley wilderness of Holy Cross Monastery feeling more centered and refreshed. God's mercies are new every morning.

I thought of the monastery bells in the days following my return. On a Wednesday evening during Advent, the church offered a quiet service of mediation and sung chant, accompanied by viola. We listened to a reading, sang, prayed, and sat among the votive candles for a long stretch of contemplative silence. For busy New Yorkers, it offered a mini-retreat—at least until the downstairs buzzer rang, noisier than the sirens from the firehouse across the street. Someone rudely stabbed at that buzzer over and over and over. Finally, it ended, only to happen again, and then again. Stab! Stab! Stab! What an unwelcome assault on our quiet time, like the sharp tines that rake at Anthony's ears in certain renderings.

I remained seated with the others but focused entirely on the buzzer and my annoyance until I realized what the noise was all about. A group of volunteers had prepared a special dinner for the shelter residents who were arriving early for the occasion. The downstairs doorbell is intentionally loud so that it can be heard anywhere in the building. We could certainly hear it up in the sanctuary. Then I remembered the monastery's angelus bell: "Hail Mary, full of grace, the Lord is with you."

Down in the basement, volunteers spread out pretty tablecloths and someone was lighting candles as we had done in the upstairs sanctuary. One by one, the young people came to the door and rang the buzzer. Hail Kimmie! Hail Lonnie! Hail Jay! Hail Zoe! Hail Ben! Hail Nikki! Hail Carlos! Hail Alleyna! Most angelus bells do not sound like buzzers, but we make do with what is given to us.

20

La Morenita

> So interesting to see "Progressive" Democrat Congresswomen, who originally came from countries whose governments are a complete and total catastrophe, the worst, most corrupt and inept anywhere in the world (if they even have a functioning government at all), now loudly and viciously telling the people of the United States, the greatest and most powerful Nation on earth, how our government is to be run. Why don't they go back and help fix the totally broken and crime infested places from which they came.

In the story of the Virgin of Guadalupe, Juan Diego, an indigenous Mexican, travels to the capital city from the countryside with a message of change for the bishop. The bishop takes a page from the White House lawn and tells him to get out of the capital city and go back to where he came from. We tell the story every Advent on the Sunday closest to December 12, the Virgin of Guadalupe's official feast date. The celebration is bilingual, rather than Spanish only, because the Mexicans who organize it want to share it widely with the community.

When a banner of the Virgin of Guadalupe appeared in our Lutheran church, some questioned her presence because many people see an image of Mary and think it's Roman Catholic. Ironically, images of Mary were already all around the sanctuary in the windows, but nobody ever remarked on those, perhaps because she looked so familiar, so white, unlike the brown-skinned Mary from Mexico who is much closer in color to the biblical Mary. I have heard people say that the narrative behind Mary in church windows is biblical while the story of the Virgin of Guadalupe is not. That might be true except that every Mary portrayed in our windows, and in most windows, appears with layers of nonbiblical symbols and interpretation. The Guadalupe is one among many, varied interpretations of Mary.

On the evening before the Guadalupe celebration, the aromas of cinnamon from the bubbling *atole*, a sweet rice drink, and shredded chicken simmering in spices greeted everyone who came through the door. Children were outside the kitchen blowing up red, white, and green balloons to tie to the ends of the pews. Before long, their fingers wore down and required help with the tying. I helped until my own fingers ached.

Upstairs, helpers strung brightly colored *papel picado* from column to column across the sanctuary. These festive banners of cut tissue paper came to us directly from Mexico thanks to those who could visit their family there, and some were purchased in East Harlem along with *pan dulce* at Mi Querido Mexico Lindo bakery. We moved La Guadalupana from her position at a side altar to the center of the church. One family, now living in Brooklyn, showed up with a Virgin of Guadalupe statue surrounded with flashing lights. Our new altar cloth was spread out with pride. Some had already come with armfuls of roses, but many more flowers would arrive tomorrow. Children ran up and down the stairs with pitchers of water to fill jars and vases set around the altar in anticipation.

While the church hummed with devotion and preparations, many people had been running with a torch, carrying a flame from the Basilica of Our Lady of Guadalupe in Mexico City all the way to St. Patrick's Cathedral here in New York. The celebration there would be much grander, but a torch had been carried here too, passed from generation to generation with love and pride, and tomorrow dozens of candles would be lit among the roses. The last task of the night was to crumple up a wide roll of brown paper to wrap around our tall wooden pulpit. Juana added a few touches of paint and suddenly, the Aztec hill of Tepeyac rose in place of the old German pulpit.

On Sunday morning, children in costume assembled to act out their story. The bishop wore one of my black clergy shirts, which was long enough on him to be a cassock. His tall, red cardboard miter kept slipping off until enough bobby pins were applied. Juan Diego arrived with his black mustache already painted on. He was outfitted in the *tilma* or poncho worn by a poor, indigenous *campesino*. One side was plain brown and the other had a radiant image of La Guadalupana taken off a T-shirt and carefully sewn into the fabric. We also had a sick uncle character whose role was to slouch in a chair looking half dead and then to jump up in renewed health when his time came. Mary wore a traditional woven skirt and a long blue veil glittering with tiny stars all around.

The children knew this story by heart. Juan Diego wandered out in the countryside on his way to a church far away, when he heard the beautiful sound of birds singing. A cell phone recording held to the microphone filled the church with birdsong. Juan Diego followed the sound to the hill of Tepeyac, where he saw a shining vision of Mary, who spoke to him with love and told him to take a message to the bishop in Mexico City to build a church closer to where he and so many others lived. Our Guadalupe's own mother remained behind in Mexico and she longed to build her life closer to her children.

The bishop, who was rather short and needed to stand on a low table to appear more imposing, refused to listen to a poor, uneducated, conquered Indian. Juan Diego had no right to be in this center of ecclesial and political power telling the bishop how to run things any more than Trump thinks a group of first-year house Democrats, who are women of color, should have a voice and vote in Washington. Juan Diego set off to tell Mary his discouraging news. Before reaching her, he discovered worse news about his uncle, who lay near death. Little girls fanned the uncle but his fever continued to climb. The Guadalupe called out to Juan Diego and told him not to worry about the uncle, who will be healed. Instead, he should continue on to Tepeyac, where he will find roses even though it was winter. He should fill his *tilma* with roses and take them to the bishop as a sign.

As Mary spoke, a little too softly for those in the back, Tepeyac bloomed with red and pink roses stuck on by little hands of every color as the prophet promised: "The wilderness and the dry land shall be glad; the desert shall rejoice and blossom" (Isaiah 35:1). The deserts of ancient Israel and Mexico met in New York City and when Juan Diego stepped out from behind the hillside, he held his *tilma* up to carry the roses. Once again, he traveled to Mexico City for an audience with the bishop, where he allowed the roses to fall at the bishop's feet. The image of the Virgin of Guadalupe was revealed on his poncho. The bishop's hand went to his mouth in shock and then he knelt in awe. He would heed Juan Diego's message and the poncho would be hung in a cathedral for millions of yearly visitors to behold. Back in Washington, Trump has not yet been brought to his knees.

After everyone took their bows, we sang *La Guadalupana*, my favorite Guadalupe song, led by an enthusiastic group of young students of mariachi music. Together, we sang the refrain: *Y eran Mexicanas, y eran Mexicanas y eran Mexicans su porte y su faz*, meaning that the appearance of Mary was Mexican. She bears the color of indigenous Mexican people and is often affectionately called *La Morenita*, the "Dark One." The children were passing on the torch of their treasured cultural heritage and history, but the story belongs to all of us because it is also deeply biblical, and surprisingly Lutheran.

Most of Luther's critique of Marian piety stemmed from his belief that the church of his day had taken Mary away from the people and held her captive in a prison of gold, distant and unreachable. Luther notes, "Among the downtrodden people, she was one of the lowliest, not a made of high station in the capital city, but a daughter of a plain man in a small village." Likewise, the vision of the Guadalupe is a vision of correction and reform for the church, reorienting the church to the margins. She appears not as the white-skinned virgin brought from Spain, but with the hair and features of an indigenous woman. She speaks the indigenous language, Nahuatl. It reminds me of Luther's insistence that the church should speak the language of the masses, not Latin, known only by an elite minority.

Not only did the Virgin of Guadalupe speak to Juan Diego in his native tongue, she gave him a powerful message to take to the bishop. The untutored peasant layman received a word to evangelize the church, like the shepherds of the Christmas story whom the angels entrusted with the message of Jesus's birth. "Who would have thought," wrote Luther, "the men whose job was tending unreasoning animals would be so praised that not a pope or bishop is worthy to hand them a cup of water?" La Morenita's message rings true down the generations to our own in a church that systemically privileges the white middle class. Women of color leaders in the Lutheran church persistently encounter the disregard experienced by the four congresswomen Trump accused of being "very racist" and "not very smart." There are many from the margins, like Juan Diego, laying their talents and energies on the line to bring a word of change to the church and to Washington. Too often, they face the same disdain that greeted Juan Diego.

And yet, these are not the only people who feel disdained. Whole communities felt disdained when Hillary Clinton consigned them to a "basket of deplorables." Many working-class, rural white people feel disdained by liberal elites. I, of course, am a liberal elite—I'm white, well-educated, live in New York City, and get the *New York Times* delivered to my door.

There are times when I may fail, but I hope to uphold the difference between a distain that extends to all those of differing opinions and experiences, which I do not want to promote, and unambiguous condemnation of positions that harm others and even endanger their lives.

One of my heroes is a friend and former intern, Jeremy Posadas, a queer person of color who teaches religion and gender studies at a small college in north Texas. One would not expect to find a person like Jeremy fitting into this very red corner of a very red state, but Jeremy has found meaning, not only in bringing new perspectives, but in listening and appreciating the perspectives of others, away from our coastal bubbles. Sure, he's experienced an anti-queer vibe at times, and he's seen his share of Confederate flags, but he's also met many queer-affirming people, people open to interracial couples, and people who don't fit into easy stereotypes. Jeremy sees a rural America left behind and suffering from the disintegration of their communities in a struggling, rural economy. He notes that rural, working-class people in both red and blue America often feel left out of the conversation by both parties.

On a day after I had attended a meeting about the difficulty of getting clergy and laypeople in metropolitan New York to take anti-racism training, I called Jeremy, just to catch up, and found myself reflecting on the morning's meeting. Jeremy said something that struck me then as ironic, but has later come to seem profound: that many people living in small, rural communities have never been offered the opportunity of anti-racism training—not in schools, churches, or workplaces—and that such opportunities are a kind of privilege in themselves, a privilege I see being rebuffed by many in blue New York.

Jeremy says, "To be part of the solution, I have to be willing to live in a place where there aren't many people like me and try to build genuine mutually respectful relationships." He's talking about small-town Texas, but I see parallels between his present work and the community-building efforts I've undertaken over the years in New York. Talking with Jeremy also makes me realize that his red-state students have more in common with Juan Diego than I first noticed. They, too, live on the margins of economic power and cultural esteem. Like Juan Diego, they face disdain before their message is fully heard.

When our Guadalupe worship ended, some stayed upstairs to take photos at our Tepeyac. Numerous baby Juan Diegos with black moustaches and mini sombreros came forward along with little girls in woven shawls and skirts topped with embroidered flowered blouses. Others hurried down to the feast where the spicy chicken would be piled on toasted tortillas along with beans, *queso*, shredded lettuce, cilantro, *salsa verde*, and *crema*. A musician played popular Mexican dance music and eventually segued into *Mi Viego San Juan* for the Puerto Ricans who felt slightly sidelined and then, Dominican salsa. A group of Chinese senior citizens had seen a flyer about the celebration and arrived to join the dancing. Now we sang to "New York, New York" as an elderly couple, both of them widowed and remarried at the church, were dancing cheek-to-cheek. Suddenly, the musician put on the Gangnam Style song, newly popular at the time, and Juan Diego busted out his gangnam moves. While so much of the fabric of our common life is unraveling, here in our church basement, a dark-skinned woman from a shit-hole country, with an anchor baby in her womb, pulled us together.

21

Morning Sickness

There was blood coming out of her eyes, out of her wherever.

I come again after nearly four decades of pastoral ministry to the story of Mary's visit to her cousin Elizabeth. When my younger self chose it as my ordination text, I identified with Mary's youthful revolutionary fire notable in the song she sings.

> My soul magnifies the Lord,
> and my spirit rejoices in God my Savior . . .
> He has brought down the powerful from their thrones,
> and lifted up the lowly;
> he has filled the hungry with good things,
> and sent the rich away empty. (Luke 1:46–47, 52–53)

I still resonate with these words. But as I age, I've begun to see myself in the older Elizabeth, and I'm noticing some new components in the story as well.

According to Luke, as soon as the angel Gabriel appears and astonishes Mary with news of her impending pregnancy, Mary hurries off to visit Elizabeth and we're given a detail that only now has begun to intrigue me: the visit lasted three months. Why does Luke mention three months? If Luke was a physician, he would surely know that the first three months are the most vulnerable time of pregnancy. A large percentage of miscarriages happen in the first trimester and many women choose not to share news of their pregnancy until those tender months have passed.

Luke would also know about morning sickness. While every body is different, morning sickness is most common during the first three months. For the majority of women, the body adjusts to the rush of hormonal changes by the end of the first trimester and morning sickness goes away. It seems that Mary hastened to reach Elizabeth before morning sickness had a chance to seriously hinder her travels. I wonder if she ended up staying three months because it took that long before she felt well enough to make the return trip. For many women, and it was certainly my experience, morning sickness during the first trimester is constant. In Spanish, the term is *malabarriga*, or evil belly.

Mary's revolutionary song—called the Magnificat—comes to us out of these three months of *malabarriga,* a time of churning upheaval in her body and in the social body she was part of. We can imagine her anxiety and uncertainty, the gossip swirling around her, leaving her vulnerable to the miscarriage of justice, the threat of community rejection, and possible death. All this is taking place in Judea, a Roman colony under the rule of Herod, whose brutal and capricious reign was itself a sort of *malabarriga* that's felt by many in Washington these days.

Just as Mary's body needed to adjust to the way it was changing, so must the church. Generational changes affect church attendance and provoke questions around worship styles, leadership styles, and what meaningful and authentic mission looks like. It's also a time of changing racial demographics that shock the system of white supremacy, both outside and inside many churches. There is fear, despair, and avoidance of environmental catastrophe. Increasing numbers of young people reject rigid binaries around gender and sexuality that were once accepted norms. Many people get queasy while absorbing Mary's words of some being brought down from positions of privilege while others are lifted up so that a true, beloved community can form.

Most of the time, feeling sick indicates that something is wrong, and we want to do everything possible to get rid of whatever is causing us to feel ill. I know quite a few churches that have closed or that are about to close because they would rather die than live through uncomfortable changes. Many people make similar choices when they cast their vote, stomaching bitter capsules of misogyny and racism if those are the price of being spared even greater, imagined discomforts. But the body's churning is not always a sign of illness. It is sometimes—as with pregnancy's morning sickness—a sign of new life. Instead of demeaning the wisdom of women's bodies, our church and our nation could learn from them.

The three months Mary spent with Elizabeth surely incorporated discomfort, but it was also a shared liminal space of pregnancy. Being a sanctuary church is like that. It's not always comfortable to live and worship in a shelter. If a gay Jamaican refugee is in the shower on Sunday morning a couple of minutes beyond his allotted time, what is the toddler arriving for Wee Worship to do when she needs the toilet? When volunteers need the undercroft on Wednesday night to set up for the following day's Thanksgiving meal that will serve nearly one thousand people, where will those who are sheltered in the same room each night stay? The answers are that we have a second bathroom, which may or may not be occupied, and the Wednesday volunteers will carry all the beds upstairs into the sanctuary for that one night. Sanctuary is not without stresses, exactly because sanctuary is an embodied way for dreams to grow in a protected space so that a different future can be born.

For Luke, who also wrote the Acts of the Apostles, three months is always such a generative time. In Acts, Luke tells us that Paul stayed in Ephesus for three months and "spoke boldly" to the people there. Then Paul stayed in Greece for three months of sanctuary, a safe place in the face of violent plots against him. Later, after the ship that was carrying him to Rome to stand trial was wrecked in a storm, Paul and his companions stayed on the island of Malta for three months, another season of sanctuary and preparation for next steps.

And so, the very young Mary seeks out the elder Elizabeth, who is in her sixth month, for a protected space, for comfort, wisdom, and support at a time when many are against her. We understand that Mary needs Elizabeth, but Elizabeth also needs Mary. Elizabeth is closer to the age of many in our pews. Elizabeth's generation is aging and their church is not birthing the new children they hoped for. According to the numbers, their church is barren. But this story sees things differently. Mary and Elizabeth carry the future together. In God's mercy, one generation needs the other.

The little one that has taken flesh in Elizabeth's aging body is intimately connected to the new life in Mary's body, and Elizabeth feels it in her belly: "For as soon as I heard the sound of your greeting, the child in my womb leaped for joy. And blessed is she who believed that there would be a fulfillment of what was spoken to her by the Lord" (Luke 1:44–45). I know this feeling. I know the joyful quickening in my soul when I see the many seminarians I've mentored graduating and getting ordained to live out their own magnificent visions. I know the flutter in my stomach as I hear their sermons and podcasts, read their writings, and witness the transformative communities they are forming. I know the leap of joy when our young congregational president greets the church, leads council meetings, organizes in the street, and mentors fellow DACA recipients.

As an older woman, I now notice this: both Mary and Elizabeth bear new life, but the older Elizabeth privileges the younger Mary's pregnancy. Elizabeth prioritizes Mary's need for hospitality and sanctuary and perhaps, most importantly, Elizabeth shows a preferential option for Mary's voice and vision over her own. I want to learn how to pattern myself after Elizabeth. She utters a word of affirmation and blessing and steps aside so that the voice of Mary may sing out. Elizabeth models a way forward for older generations in the church: sometimes we must stand down, sit down, and be quiet, so that the voices and visions of another generation can be heard.

In Advent Wee Worship, I handed out magnifying glasses to help us think about what it means when Mary sings: "My soul magnifies the Lord" (Luke 1:46). It's easy to magnify all the other things that loom large and claim our full attention while the promises and words of God recede to the peripheral edges of our awareness, but Mary and Elizabeth model a different way. Elizabeth allows the tiny, kicking feet of John the Baptist to become a prophetic witness heralding the presence of Christ in Mary. Mary can't yet feel any elbows or feet, perhaps just a faint flutter. She sings of a future too small to see, taking shape in her womb. Mary lifts up truth in a world that magnifies so many lies. Advent reminds us to look for the small flutters.

The Brazilian theologian Ruben Alves describes such embryonic hope like this:

> Hope is that presentiment that the imagination is more real, and reality less real, than we had thought. It is the sensation that the last word does not belong to the brutality of facts with their oppression and repression. It is the suspicion that reality is far more complex than realism would have us believe, that the frontiers of the possible are not determined by the limits of the present, and that miraculously and surprisingly, life is readying the creative event that will open the way to freedom and resurrection.

Each Advent, Trinity hosts a craft night for children to come and eat pizza and make Christmas ornaments. In preparation, we spread newspapers over the tables to catch the glitter and glue and make clean-up easier. As the papers went down, I noticed the news they bore, unfit for children: "Bomb Threats Sweeping the U.S.," "The Earth's Shell Has Cracked, and We're Drifting on the Pieces," "Deaths in Yemen," "Homelessness Rises Despite Strong Economy," "White Supremacist Gang Attacked Black D. J.," and "Trump Officials Plan to Rescind Obama-Era School Discipline Policies"—because in the wake of the Parkland school murders, instead of gun control, Betsy DeVos wanted to reverse efforts to ensure that minority students are not unfairly disciplined. I hoped none of the children coming would notice and, of course, they didn't. They focused on making angels and decorating cookies and turning candy canes into reindeer and glitter-bombing snowflakes.

On Christmas Eve, we sing the beloved carol "Joy to the World," including verse 3:

> No more let sin and sorrow grow,
> nor thorns infest the ground;
> he comes to make his blessings flow
> far as the curse is found,
> far as the curse is found,
> far as, far as the curse is found.

The thorn-infested ground was spread out in front of our children by way of those grim newspapers and they would shortly go outside to face it directly. Did those few hours of warm sanctuary and glittery happiness matter? For my part, I'm with Mary and Elizabeth. I say yes. I choose to magnify the flutters.

POSTSCRIPT

Sanctuary

> Getting more dangerous. "Caravans" coming.
>
> Criminals and unknown Middle Easterners mixed in.
>
> Republicans must go to Nuclear Option to pass tough laws now.

On the Sunday following my trip to the border, I announced that we would share the peace using only our pinkies. Sharing the peace is a tradition in many churches that occurs at a chosen moment in the liturgy. In my church it occurs after the prayers and before the offering. In some churches people stand up from their seats and extend a greeting to those they can reach. The greeting might be a handshake, a hug, or a nod with the words "peace be with you" depending on the congregation and the preference of each person, recognizing that some do not wish to be hugged or touched at all. At Trinity, sharing the peace is a joyous, free-flowing moment in worship with people moving around the church to hug, smile, and shake hands with as many as possible. I knew that instructing people to use only their pinkies was going to be weird, as it was for me when I first encountered it.

A few days before traveling home from the border, I attended a worship service with La Iglesia Fronteriza, the Border Church, at Friendship Park. Located between San Diego and Tijuana, the park was founded in 1971 as a symbol of friendship between Mexico and the United States. Within an enclosed area, under the supervision of the United States Border Patrol, people from both sides of the border came together for picnics and other shared events. In 1994, amid widespread hysteria about unauthorized immigration between San Diego and Tijuana, a fourteen-mile-long fence was constructed on the border as part of Operation Gatekeeper.

Operation Gatekeeper was launched under the Clinton administration with a goal of stopping immigrants from crossing the busy San Diego–Tijuana border. New fencing was built, increased electronic surveillance was installed, and two hundred additional border patrol agents were hired to guard the area. Instead of deterring immigration, it led people to take a wide detour through treacherous desert and mountain areas leading to more deaths due to dehydration and sunstroke in the summer or freezing in winter months.

I visited one group, Humane Borders, that placed water barrels in the desert to help prevent such deaths. After Trump took office, it became routine for border agents to vandalize these containers, shooting holes in them so that life-saving water drained out into the sand. In 2018, Scott Warren, a volunteer who left water for migrants, was arrested on felony harboring charges. Warren was at a location called "the Barn," in a deadly stretch of desert, but this barn was not a structure at all. It was simply an area with an assortment of bins containing water bottles, some food, and other supplies. Shortly before his arrest, Warren released a video he'd filmed of border agents destroying jugs that together held thousands of gallons of water. When he was seen at the Barn giving supplies to two immigrants assumed to be undocumented, Warren was arrested. His trial ended with a hung jury.

After Operation Gatekeeper went into effect, the picnics at Friendship Park stopped. Nonetheless, while people could no longer meet for gatherings, they could still pass family photos, favorite treats, and other objects through the new barriers to those separated from them. They could reach through to hold hands, stroke a loved one's face, and even share a kiss until a new mesh fence was added with tiny holes preventing anything from passing through. But even this was not enough of a barrier as people could still approach the fence and speak through it. In 2009, the Department of Homeland Security constructed a second, parallel fence that stretches into the Pacific Ocean and includes barbed wire, sensors, surveillance cameras, and underwater spikes to stop swimmers. Today, there's a no-man's-land between the two sides. You can barely see people gathered across the emptiness on the other side. In order for the Border Church to worship together, a leader on each side hooks up their phone to a loudspeaker.

As an opening confession, we were invited to place our hands on the hard, metal slats of the wall, feeling the cold embodiment of the sin that divides us from one another and from God. The pastor then directed us to look up into the boundless, blue sky above as he offered words of forgiveness and proclaimed: *En el cielo no hay muros*, "In the sky, there are no walls." The Spanish word for "sky" is also the word for "heaven."

Here on earth, my favorite part of that worship was the sharing of the peace. The Border Church congregation was told to share the peace using only our pinkie fingers. I thought this was peculiar and asked about it when the service ended. The pastor explained that during the brief period when people could still approach the thick mesh fence, but the holes were too small to pass any objects through, divided families and friends could touch the tips of their pinkies in what they called a fingertip kiss. Today, the Border Church remembers that moment in time whenever they gather. For me, it also felt like a way to recall the power and importance of even small connections across all the prejudices, structures, and systems that would keep us apart, something that does not require travel to our southern border.

My church, the Evangelical Lutheran Church in America, was the first denomination to officially declare itself a Sanctuary Church. What does that mean? It will be worked out on the ground in individual congregations. Surely committees will form and create lists of options suggested for study, worship, and action. My hope for this book is to contribute to the sanctuary conversation and to inspire and encourage the multiplying of real brick-and-mortar sanctuary spaces among us. I hope that the stories passed on from a small and scrappy sanctuary church will serve as little openings that allow the reader to be touched by the unlikely reunions that occur despite the dividing walls we face.

When I visited Humane Borders, I saw that their water barrels were marked with blue flags raised on thirty-foot poles, easily visible for miles around the flat, desert terrain. All churches do not, and need not, have tall steeples, but it occurs to me that our communities and steeples should be like that, clear signs that say: Here is water. Here is welcome. Here is life.

NOTES

I have used the New Revised Standard version of the Bible for all Scripture quotations. All epigraphs are quotes from Donald Trump.

1. PUTTING HEROD BACK IN CHRISTMAS

"I play to people's fantasies." Donald J. Trump with Tony Schwartz, *Trump: The Art of the Deal* (New York: Random, 1987), 58.

"The beauty of me is that I'm very rich." Ashleigh Banfield, Rich McHugh, and Suzan Clarke, "Donald Trump Would Spend $600 Million of His Own Money On Presidential Bid," *ABC News*, March 17, 2011, https://abcnews.go.com/Politics/donald-trump-president-trump-weighs-sheen-palin-obama/story?id=13154163.

"The world was gloomy . . ." Donald J. Trump (@realDonaldTrump), "The world was gloomy before I won - there was no hope. Now the market is up nearly 10% and Christmas spending is over a trillion dollars!," Twitter, December 26, 2016, 6:32 p.m., https://twitter.com/realdonaldtrump/status/813527932165558273?lang=en.

"I have a very good brain." Meghan Keneally, "President Trump Has Called Himself Smart Six Times Before," *ABC News*, January 8, 2018, https://abcnews.go.com/Politics/president-trump-called-smart-six-times-before/story?id=52209712.

"My twitter has become so powerful . . ." Donald J. Trump (@realDonaldTrump), "My twitter has become so powerful that I can actually make my enemies tell the truth," Twitter, October 17, 2012, 11:06 a.m., https://twitter.com/realdonaldtrump/status/258584864163500033?lang=en.

"The people following me are very passionate." Dara Lind, "Donald Trump's Appalling Reaction to a Hate Crime Committed in His Name," *Vox*, updated August 21, 2015, https://www.vox.com/2015/8/20/9182169/trump-hate-crime.

"Deportation Time." California News Wire Services, "Group of Oceanside Students Design Deportation-Themed Board Game," *Patch Media*, October 1, 2018, https://patch.com/california/oceanside-camppendleton/group-oceanside-students-design-deportation-themed-board-game.

"Normal fear . . ." Martin Luther King Jr., *Strength to Love* (Minneapolis, MN: Fortress Press, 2010), 124.

"I like money." Randy Haspel, "Beatitudes: The Gospel of Donald J. Trump," *Memphis Flyer*, January 9, 2018, https://www.memphisflyer.com/memphis/beatitudes-the-gospel-of-donald-j-trump/Content?oid=10511603.

"When people wrong you . . ." Michael Kruse and Noah Weiland, "Donald Trump's Greatest Self-Contradictions," *Politico*, May 5, 2016, https://www.politico.com/magazine/story/2016/05/donald-trump-2016-contradictions-213869.

2. Jesus in a Dog Cage on *Good Morning America*

"Now you don't get separated . . ." Kimberly Kindy, Nick Miroff, and Maria Sacchetti, "Trump says ending family separation practice was a 'disaster' that led to surge in border crossings," *Washington Post*, April 28, 2019, https://www.washingtonpost.com/politics/trump-says-ending-family-separation-practice-was-a-disaster-that-led-to-surge-in-border-crossings/2019/04/28/73e9da14-69c8-11e9-a66d-a82d3f3d96d5_story.html.

"The world is charged . . ." Gerard Manley Hopkins, "God's Grandeur," in *The Major Works, Including All the Poems and Selected Prose*, ed. Catherine Phillips (Oxford: Oxford University Press, 1986), 128.

"On Christmas Morning . . ." Tim Graham, "On Christmas Morning, Lutheran Pastor on ABC Compares Illegal Aliens to Jesus and His Family," MRC, *NewsBusters*, December 26, 2018, https://www.newsbusters.org/blogs/nb/tim-graham/2018/12/26/christmas-morning-lutheran-pastor-abc-compares-illegal-aliens-jesus.

3. Bedbugs, Condoms, Frankincense, and Myrrh

"Sorry, there is no STAR on the stage tonight." Donald J. Trump (@realDonaldTrump), "Sorry, there is no STAR on the stage tonight!," Twitter, October 13, 2015, 10:02 p.m. https://twitter.com/realdonaldtrump/status/654114913888174081?lang=en.

"Little lamb, Who made thee . . ." William Blake, *Songs of Innocence and of Experience* (Oxford: Oxford University Press, 1970), 134.

"O Morning Star, how fair and bright!" *Evangelical Lutheran Worship* (Minneapolis, MN: Augsburg Fortress, 2006), 308. Text copyright 1978 Lutheran Book of Worship, admin. Augsburg Fortress. Reproduced by permission.

"Star of wonder, star of light . . ." *With One Voice: A Lutheran Resource for Worship* (Minneapolis, MN: Augsburg Fortress, 1995), 646.

4. Poor Doors

"First of all, I am a great Christian . . ." John Santucci, "Donald Trump's Message: 'Let Me Win Iowa,'" ABC News, October 27, 2015, https://abcnews.go.com/Politics/trumps-message-iowa-great-christian/story?id=34781048.

"No one ever said that the goal was full integration." Pat Regnier, "NYC Apartment Building Will Have Separate Door for Lower Rent Tenants. What's Up With That?," *Money*, July 22, 2014, http://money.com/money/3018706/separate-entrances-affordable-housing-new-york-city/.

At the time, I never imagined that Extell, Trump, and Chinese . . . Lachlan Markay, "Giant Claims, Tiny Evidence: Inside the Trump Legal Playbook," *The Daily Beast*, June 22, 2017, https://www.thedailybeast.com/giant-claims-tiny-evidence-inside-the-trump-legal-playbook.

Before the 1978 World Cup . . . Will Hersey, "Remembering Argentina 1978: The Dirtiest World Cup Of All Time," *Esquire*, June 14, 2018, https://www.esquire.com/uk/culture/a21454856/argentina-1978-world-cup/.

. . . opportunity to study with Gustavo Gutierrez . . . Gustavo Gutierrez, *We Drink from Our Own Wells: The Spiritual Journey of a People* (Maryknoll, NY: Orbis Books, 1984).

"The denunciation of injustice . . ." Gustavo Gutierrez, *A Theology of*

Liberation: History, Politics and Salvation (Maryknoll, NY: Orbis Books, 1988), 79.

A few months earlier at a Florida rally . . . Peter Baker and Michael D. Shear, "El Paso Shooting Suspect's Manifesto Echoes Trump's Language," *New York Times*, August 4, 2019, https://www.nytimes.com/2019/08/04/us/politics/trump-mass-shootings.html.

5. That None May Be Lost

"What you're seeing and what you're reading is not what's happening." "Donald Trump: 'What you're seeing and what you're reading is not what's happening,'" BBC News, July 25, 2018, https://www.bbc.com/news/av/world-us-canada-44959340/donald-trump-what-you-re-seeing-and-what-you-re-reading-is-not-what-s-happening.

In *Life Together* . . . Dietrich Bonhoeffer, *Life Together* (New York: Harper and Row, 1954), 97.

In the words of . . . then Manhattan Borough President . . . Heidi Neumark, *Breathing Space: A Spiritual Journey in the South Bronx* (Boston: Beacon Press, 2003), 15. For more on Robert Moses, see Robert Caro, *The Power Broker* (New York: Vintage Books, Random House, 1975).

6. Whiter Than Snow

"I have a great relationship with the blacks." Garance Franke-Ruta, "Donald Trump: 'I Have a Great Relationship with the Blacks,'" *The Atlantic*, April 14, 2011, https://www.theatlantic.com/politics/archive/2011/04/donald-trump-i-have-a-great-relationship-with-the-blacks/237332/.

For a more recent, in-depth perspective on race and color in worship, see Lenny Duncan, *Dear Church: A Love Letter from a Black Preacher to the Whitest Denomination in the US* (Minneapolis, MN: Fortress Press, 2019).

7. Suffer the Little Children

"The beauty that's being taken out of our cities, towns and parks . . ." Donald J. Trump (@realDonaldTrump), "the beauty that is being taken out of our cities, towns and parks will be greatly missed and never able to be comparably replaced!," Twitter, August 17, 2017, 9:21 a.m. https://twitter.com/realdonaldtrump/status/898172999945392131?lang=en.

1908 was also the height of German colonial rule in Africa. David Olusoga and Casper W. Erichsen, *The Kaiser's Holocaust: Germany's Forgotten Genocide* (London: Faber and Faber, 2010).

. . . the indigenous Lenape people . . . Eric W. Sanderson, *Mannahatta: A Natural History of New York City* (New York: Harry N. Abrams, 2009), 103–35.

The Washington National Cathedral has removed . . . Emily Cochrane, "National Cathedral to Remove Windows Honoring Confederate Generals," *New York Times*, September 6, 2017, https://www.nytimes.com/2017/09/06/us/politics/washington-national-cathedral-stained-glass-confederate-lee.html.

In one of Yale University's dining halls . . . Zoe Greenberg, "Yale Drops Case against Worker Who Smashed Window Depicting Slaves," *New York Times*, July 12, 2016, https://www.nytimes.com/2016/07/13/nyregion/yale-worker-john-c-calhoun-window-slaves.html.

8. Leap before You Look

"This is about safety. It has nothing to do with religion." John Santucci, "Donald Trump Insists Muslim Ban Is about Safety, Not Religion," ABC News, December 9, 2015, https://abcnews.go.com/Politics/donald-trump-insists-muslim-ban-safety-religion/story?id=35666498.

It was the last Sunday of June in 2004 . . . Andrew Jacobs, "For Young Gays on the Streets, Survival Comes Before Pride; Few Beds for Growing Class of Homeless," *New York Times*, June 27, 2004, https://www.nytimes.com/2004/06/27/nyregion/for-young-gays-streets-survival-comes-before-pride-few-beds-for-growing-class.html.

I wanted to mention Mexico's rich history among its indigenous cultures. Marc Lacey, "A Lifestyle Distinct: The Muxe of Mexico," *New York Times*, December 6, 2008, https://www.nytimes.com/2008/12/07/weekinreview/07lacey.html.

"Leap Before You Look," . . . W. H. Auden, *Auden: Poems* (New York: Alfred A. Knopf, 1995), 113.

9. Measuring Up

"Hello Miss Piggy, Hello Miss Housekeeping." "Alicia Machado: Ex-Miss Universe Claims Trump Called Her 'Miss Piggy,'" BBC News, September 27, 2016, https://www.bbc.com/news/world-us-canada-37488060.

. . . after their president publicly called the Venezuelan Miss Universe "Miss Piggy." Michael Barbaro and Megan Twohey, "Shamed and Angry: Alicia Machado, a Miss Universe Mocked by Donald Trump," *New York Times*, September 27, 2016, https://www.nytimes.com/2016/09/28/us/politics/alicia-machado-donald-trump.html.

Some scholars believe that Luke's story of Martha and Mary . . . Elisabeth Schüssler Fiorenza, *Discipleship of Equals: A Critical Feminist Ekklesia-logy of Liberation* (New York: Crossroad Publishing, 1993), 202–5.

The theologian Paul Tillich preached . . . Paul Tillich, *The New Being* (London: D. M. Brown, 1956), 152–60.

Dorothee Sölle, the German liberation theologian, writes . . . Dorothee Sölle, *The Silent Cry: Mysticism and Resistance* (Minneapolis, MN: Fortress Press, 2001), 2.

"Never forget," says Cornel West . . . Bell Hooks and Cornel West, *Breaking Bread: Insurgent Black Intellectual Life* (Abingdon, UK: Routledge, 2016), 55.

She acquired a set of books that included *The Shape of the Liturgy* . . . Dom Gregory Dix, *The Shape of the Liturgy* (London: Dacre Press, Adam & Charles Black, 1945).

10. Night of Betrayal

"We're rounding 'em up in a very humane way, in a very nice way." Scott Pelley, "Trump Gets Down to Business on 60 Minutes," CBS News, September 27, 2015, https://www.cbsnews.com/news/donald-trump-60-minutes-scott-pelley/.

11. Credible Fear

"It's a big fat con job, folks." "Donald Trump Calls Asylum Claims a 'Big Fat Con Job,'" *Newsweek*, March 29, 2019, https://www.youtube.com/watch?v=OKpdCuHdhZE.

12. Pupusas at the Tomb

"We're going to build a wall, folks." "Trump on Immigration: 'That Wall Will Go Up So Fast Your Head Will Spin,'" Grabien, August 22, 2016, https://grabien.com/story.php?id=62879.

As Clarence Jordan once said . . . Clarence Jordan, "Voice of the Day," *Sojourners,* April 10, 2013, https://sojo.net/articles/voice-day-clarence-jordan-0.

The Talmudic scholar Rabbi Yohanan . . . Erica Brown, "Sanctuary Eyes: Why Do Synagogue Sanctuaries Have Windows?" *My Jewish Learning,* www.myjewishlearning.com/article/sanctuary-eyes/. Accessed December 3, 2019.

13. Dance Party

In December of 2017, the Centers for Disease Control and Prevention . . . Sheila Kaplan and Donald G. McNeil Jr., "Uproar Over Purported Ban at C.D.C. of Words Like 'Fetus,'" *New York Times,* December 16, 2017, https://www.nytimes.com/2017/12/16/health/cdc-trump-banned-words.html.

14. Better Than Dolls

"Why are we having all these people from shit hole countries come here . . . ?" Eli Watkins and Abby Phillip, "Trump Decries Immigrants from 'Shithole Countries' Coming to US," CNN, January 12, 2018, https://www.cnn.com/2018/01/11/politics/immigrants-shithole-countries-trump/index.html.

He marked Pentecost Monday of 2017 . . . "Timeline of the Donald Trump Presidency," *Wikipedia, The Free Encyclopedia*, https://en.wikipedia

.org/w/index.php?title=Timeline_of_the_Donald_Trump_presidency&oldid=938426536. Accessed December 3, 2019.

15. Team Effort

"Here's the thing. I don't have teams . . ." Shannon Pettypiece, "Trump Dismisses Need for Impeachment Advisers: 'I'm the Team,'" NBC News, October 25, 2019, https://www.nbcnews.com/politics/white-house/trump-dismisses-need-impeachment-advisers-i-m-team-n1072086.

"Believing in the Trinity means . . ." Leonardo Boff, *Holy Trinity, Perfect Community* (Maryknoll, NY: Orbis Books, 2000), xvi.

In the words of theologian Catherine Mowry LaCugna . . . Catherine Mowry LaCugna, *God for Us: The Trinity and Christian Life* (San Francisco: HarperSanFrancisco, 1993), 399.

"When the church forgets the source that gives it birth . . ." Boff, *Holy Trinity*, 67.

". . . present in time and under shadows . . ." Boff, *Holy Trinity*, 108.

16. Numbers

"I turn on one of the networks, and they show an empty field . . ." Politico Staff, "Full Text: Trump, Pence Remarks at CIA Headquarters," *Politico*, January 21, 2017, https://www.politico.com/story/2017/01/full-text-trump-pence-remarks-cia-headquarters-233978.

Trump's eyes were aglisten with the numbers: . . . Charlie May, "'What a Crowd, What a Turnout': Trump Boasts of Crowd Size during Hurricane Harvey Tour," *Salon*, August 29, 2017, www.salon.com/2017/08/29/what-a-crowd-what-a-turnout-trump-boasts-of-crowd-size-during-hurricane-harvey-tour/.

Soon after Trump took office, the questions were removed . . . "Donald Trump," *GLAAD.org*, www.glaad.org/tap/donald-trump. Accessed December 3, 2019.

Similarly, the Department of Justice has sought to raise the age . . . Richard Ferraro, "GLAAD Partners with Our Families Count to Promote LGBT Visibility in the U.S. Census," *GLAAD.org*, November 10, 2009, https://

www.glaad.org/releases/glaad-partners-our-families-count-promote-lgbt-visibility-us-census.

The Secretary of Education, Betsy DeVos . . . Brad Kutner, "Advocates Take Up Fight to Track Bullying of LGBT Youth," *Courthouse News Service*, September 20, 2019, www.courthousenews.com/advocates-take-up-fight-to-track-bullying-of-lgbt-youth/.

Such data helped the government round up and imprison Japanese Americans . . . J. R. Minkel, "Confirmed: The U.S. Census Bureau Gave Up Names of Japanese-Americans in WW II," *Scientific American*, March 30, 2007, www.scientificamerican.com/article/confirmed-the-us-census-b/.

"Underground Lives: The Sunless World of Immigrants in Queens . . ." Nikita Stewart, Ryan Christopher Jones, Sergio Peçanha, Jeffrey Furticella, and Josh Williams, "Underground Lives: The Sunless World of Immigrants in Queens," *New York Times*, October 23, 2019, https://www.nytimes.com/interactive/2019/10/23/nyregion/basements-queens-immigrants.html.

As recently as 1924, the *American Bar Association Journal* . . . Henry Clark, "And Zelophehad Had Daughters," *American Bar Association Journal* 10, no. 2 (Feb. 1924): 133–34.

. . . there were heated debates in 1930 . . . Margo J. Anderson, *The American Census: A Social History*, 2nd ed. (New Haven, CT: Yale University Press, 2015), 156–66.

17. Autumnal Saints

"I believe that there's a change in weather and I think it changes both ways." "Trump Says 'Climate Change Goes Both Ways,'" BBC News, June 5, 2019, https://www.bbc.com/news/world-us-canada-48531019.

"The constant attacks on science and facts . . ." "Science under Trump: Voices of Scientists across 16 Federal Agencies," *Union of Concerned Scientists*, August 7, 2018, https://www.ucsusa.org/resources/science-under-trump.

"We are Christians with different theological and political . . ." The Golden Rule 2020, National Institute for Civil Discourse, https://goldenrule2020.org/. Accessed December 3, 2019.

In his letter to white moderate clergy, King answered the complaints . . . Martin Luther King Jr., *A Testament of Hope: The Essential Writings and*

Speeches, ed. James M. Washington (San Francisco: HarperSanFrancisco, 2003), 289.

Martin of Tours lived in the fourth century. Silvia Vecchini, *Saint Martin of Tours* (London: Catholic Truth Society, 2007), 3–21.

18. Crown Him with Tear Gas

"Thank you to Wayne Allyn Root for the very nice words." Donald J. Trump (@realDonaldTrump), ". . . like he's the King of Israel. They love him like he is the second coming of God. . . But American Jews don't know him or like him. They don't even know what they're doing or saying anymore. It makes no sense! But that's OK, if he keeps doing what he's doing, he's good for . . ." Twitter, August 21, 2019, 7:34 a.m., https://twitter.com/realdonaldtrump/status/1164138796205654016?lang=en.

Before he moved to Washington, he lived in a $100 million . . . Talia Avakian, "The $100-million Penthouse Where Donald Trump's Family Lives in New York City," *Travel and Leisure,* November 16, 2016, https://www.travelandleisure.com/culture-design/architecture-design/trump-tower-donald-trump-penthouse.

The Christian right likes to compare Trump to King Cyrus . . . Katherine Stewart, "Why Trump Reigns as King Cyrus," *New York Times*, December 31, 2018, https://www.nytimes.com/2018/12/31/opinion/trump-evangelicals-cyrus-king.html.

"Thank you to Wayne Allyn Root . . ." Donald J. Trump (@realDonaldTrump), "Thank you to Wayne Allyn Root for the very nice words. 'President Trump is the greatest President for Jews and for Israel in the history of the world, not just America, he is the best President for Israel in the history of the world . . . and the Jewish people in Israel love him.' . . . ," Twitter, August 21, 2019, 7:34 a.m., https://twitter.com/realdonaldtrump/status/1164138795475881986?lang=en.

In 1925, in Italy, where the pope lived . . . Kevin D. Williamson, "Christ the King, King of Kings," *National Review*, November 26, 2017, https://www.nationalreview.com/2017/11/christ-king-secular-tyrants-20th-century-catholic-church-united-states/.

On Christ the King Sunday of 2018 . . . "Timeline of the Donald Trump Presidency," *Wikipedia, The Free Encyclopedia*, https://en.wikipedia.org

/w/index.php?title=Timeline_of_the_Donald_Trump_presidency&oldid=938426536. Accessed December 3, 2019.

19. Angelus

"I am your voice!" "Fact Check: Donald Trump's Republican Convention Speech, Annotated," NPR, July 21, 2016, https://www.npr.org/2016/07/21/486883610/fact-check-donald-trumps-republican-convention-speech-annotated.

At the head of this who's who list is Emperor Tiberius. "Tiberius," *Wikipedia, The Free Encyclopedia*, https://en.wikipedia.org/w/index.php?title=Tiberius&oldid=939940936. Accessed December 3, 2019.

Herod chose to design the baths of Jewish purification . . . I am in debt to Hal Taussig (pastor, teacher, and writer) for this insight.

Trappist monk Thomas Merton described these hermits . . . Thomas Merton, *The Wisdom of the Desert* (New York: New Directions, 1960), 5–6.

Merton could see that "the great travelers and colonizers of the Renaissance" . . . Merton, *The Wisdom of the Desert*, 11–12.

. . . my favorite being the devil lobster . . . Daniel Mallory Ortberg, "Paintings of the Temptation of Saint Anthony That Fundamentally Misunderstand the Concept of Temptation," *The Toast*, May 26, 2015, https://the-toast.net/2015/05/26/paintings-of-the-temptation-of-saint-anthony-that-fundamentally-misunderstand-the-concept-of-temptation/.

20. La Morenita

"So interesting to see 'Progressive' Democrat Congresswomen . . ." Donald J. Trump (@realDonaldTrump), "So interesting to see 'Progressive, Democrat Congresswomen, who originally came from countries whose governments are a complete and total catastrophe, the worst, most corrupt and inept anywhere in the world (if they even have a functioning government at all), now loudly. . . ," Twitter, July 14, 2019, 8:27 a.m. https://twitter.com/realdonaldtrump/status/1150381394234941448?lang=en.

"Among the downtrodden people . . ." Martin Luther, *The Martin Luther Christmas Book*, trans. and ed. Roland Herbert Bainton (Philadelphia, PA: Fortress Press, 1948), 20.

"Who would have thought . . ." Luther, *The Martin Luther Christmas Book*, 43.

21. Morning Sickness

"There was blood coming out of her eyes, out of her wherever." Philip Rucker, "Trump Says Fox's Megyn Kelly Had 'Blood Coming Out of Her Wherever,'" *Washington Post*, August 18, 2015, https://www.washingtonpost.com/news/post-politics/wp/2015/08/07/trump-says-foxs-megyn-kelly-had-blood-coming-out-of-her-wherever/.

"Hope is that presentiment . . ." Leonardo Boff, *Passion of Christ, Passion of the World* (Maryknoll, NY: Orbis Books, 1987), 124.

22. Postscript: Sanctuary

"Getting more dangerous." Mark Moore, "Trump Claims Migrant Caravan Contains 'Unknown Middle Easterners,'" *New York Post*, October 22, 2018, https://nypost.com/2018/10/22/trump-claims-migrant-caravan-contains-unknown-middle-easterners/.

"Republicans must go to Nuclear Option . . ." "In Easter Rant, Trump Urges GOP to Use 'Nuclear Option' on 'Dumb Immigration Laws,'" *Daily Beast*, April 1, 2018, https://www.thedailybeast.com/in-easter-rant-trump-urges-gop-to-use-nuclear-option-on-dumb-immigration-laws.

Located between San Diego and Tijuana, the park was founded in 1971 . . . "Friendship Park (San Diego–Tijuana)," *Wikipedia, The Free Encyclopedia*, https://en.wikipedia.org/w/index.php?title=Friendship_Park_(San_Diego%E2%80%93Tijuana)&oldid=932130372. Accessed December 3, 2019.

Operation Gatekeeper was launched under the Clinton administration . . . "Operation Gatekeeper," *Wikipedia, The Free Encyclopedia*, https://en.wikipedia.org/w/index.php?title=Operation_Gatekeeper&oldid=929486215. Accessed December 3, 2019.

In 2018, Scott Warren, a volunteer who left water . . . Miriam Jordan, "An Arizona Teacher Helped Migrants. Jurors Couldn't Decide If It Was a Crime," *New York Times*, June 11, 2019, https://www.nytimes.com/2019/06/11/us/scott-warren-arizona-deaths.html.